Teaching the Selected Works of Katherine Paterson

The Young Adult Novels in the Classroom Series

When former Heinemann–Boynton/Cook editor Peter Stillman first conceived the Young Adult Literature (YAL) series in 1990 and asked me to be the series editor, I was excited to be part of such an innovative endeavor. At that time there were few professional books available for teachers who wanted to bring young adult literature into their classrooms, and Heinemann was the first publisher making a concerted effort to fill this need. Seventeen years and many books later, under the direction of Heinemann Executive Editor Lisa Luedeke, the series continues to inform and assist teachers at the middle school, high school, and college levels as they read with and teach to their students the best works that the field of young adult literature has to offer.

The Heinemann YAL Series takes another step forward with the book you hold in your hands. This subseries on teaching the works of specific young adult authors is designed to help you incorporate young adult literature into your curriculum, providing ideas and lessons that you may use and offering examples of classroom-tested student work, lesson plans, and discussion as an impetus to designing your own lessons and developing your own ideas in accordance with your students' needs.

Over the years, many teachers in my graduate young adult literature classes have asked me how to convince administrators and parents that young adult literature is worthy of a place in the curriculum alongside the classics and other commonly taught literary works. In response I have shown them how to write rationales for specific books, how to design lesson plans and units that satisfy state and national standards, how to deal with censorship, and how to become connoisseurs of young adult literature themselves. I hope that the books in this subseries, by focusing on specific authors of young adult literature and highlighting the successful work of teachers with this genre, will inspire confidence in you to bring these extraordinary works into your curriculum, not just as a bridge to the classics, but as literary works in their own right.

—Virginia R. Monseau

Teaching the Selected Works of Robert Cormier

Teaching the Selected Works of Mildred D. Taylor

Teaching the Selected Works of Katherine Paterson

Teaching the Selected Works of Walter Dean Myers

Teaching the Selected Works of Gary Paulsen (forthcoming)

Teaching the Selected Works of Chris Crutcher (forthcoming)

Teaching the Selected Works of Katherine Paterson

Lois Thomas Stover

HEINEMANN
PORTSMOUTH, NH

Heinemann
A division of Reed Elsevier Inc.
361 Hanover Street
Portsmouth, NH 03801–3912
www.heinemann.com

Offices and agents throughout the world

Library of Congress Cataloging-in-Publication Data
Stover, Lois T.
    Teaching the selected works of Katherine Paterson / Lois Thomas Stover.
        p. cm. — (Young adult novels in the classroom series)
    Includes bibliographical references.
    ISBN-13: 978-0-325-00791-5
    ISBN-10: 0-325-00791-8
    1. Paterson, Katherine—Study and teaching. 2. Paterson, Katherine—Criticism and interpretation. 3. Young adult fiction, American—Study and teaching.   I. Title.

PS3566.A779Z86 2007
813'.54—dc22   2007016381

Editor: Virginia R. Monseau
Production service: Melissa L. Inglis
Production coordination: Vicki Kasabian
Cover design: Night & Day Design
Typesetter: Tom Allen, Pear Graphic Design
Manufacturing: Louise Richardson

Printed in the United States of America on acid-free paper
11 10 09 08 07   VP   1 2 3 4 5

This project would not have come into being without the guidance of series editor, Ginger Monseau, or without the effort, time, and energy given to it by the incredible teachers, Mary Christensen, Lou D'Ambrosio, Betsy Gardiner, and Kathy Slingland. Hal Foster read and provided feedback from the heart; David Finkelman calmed me when I panicked over details and deadlines; and Melissa Inglis was a patient and gracious editor. To these individuals I owe much gratitude. And many thanks to the Educational Studies Department at St. Mary's College of Maryland for providing financial support for this project.

CONTENTS

My Journey with Katherine Paterson
Discovering and Rediscovering Paterson

The currents of three personal circumstances have, in their confluence, launched me into writing this book about teaching the novels of one of the most beloved and celebrated authors writing for children and young adults today: Katherine Paterson. Many years before I became a teacher educator, I was a voracious reader who landed the perfect after-school job. I was hired to shelve books in the children's section of our town's library the summer before my last year of high school. The library itself was an incredible structure, built of stone, with leaded windows, and complete with a turret in which the stairs led to the upper floor, where the children's collection was housed. What a treat it was to be able to spend my working hours in this magical place, which felt like a treehouse given the way the windows opened—no central air conditioning back then—onto the limbs of stately oaks and maples that shaded the benches nestled under the sills. As I was putting away the returned titles, I'd often sneak a read, settling down with a title that looked particularly interesting and gobbling up the words on the page.

During that year, I came upon the newly published *The Sign of the Chrysanthemum*. The blurb on the jacket told me that the book, Paterson's first, was set in medieval Japan, and I was immediately hooked, having a long-standing interest in medieval history and a curiosity about Japan in general. I was further intrigued by the plot summary with its descriptions of the samurai code and the quest motif. Over the next few workdays, I managed to read the entire book in moments stolen from my shelving duties. I found myself thinking about Muna, wondering what was going to happen next to him, instead of worrying about the characters in the novel I was reading for my twelfth-grade honors seminar class on British literature: *The Mayor of Casterbridge*. I was a good student; I liked to read; I enjoyed conversations about books with my friends and even in my English classes. But it was in the children's section of the West Chester, Pennsylvania, public library that my love of books was most nourished during my senior year.

The books with young adult characters housed in that area of the library were the books that grabbed me, that kept me reading because of the way I could identify with the characters immediately, on an intuitive, emotional level that was not often replicated when I was plodding through the required fare of my English class. Muna, whose name means *No Name*, was in search of his identity, seeking to answer the classic question of all young adults, "Who am I?" As I was making the transition from high school honors student known in our small town as the daughter of Bud and Grace, as the granddaughter of William and Maude, as the cousin of Bob and George, Tom and Wayne, as the sister of Davis, as a member of the Methodist Church choir, the high school's Drama Club, orchestra, and chamber singers, I was chafing at the bit to figure out who I was outside that context. Traveling with Muna as he searched for his father, and for a name to call his own, was much more compelling reading than almost anything I was handed at school. Ever since that experience with *The Sign of the Chrysanthemum*, I have been a fan of Katherine Paterson's.

I went off to college, majored in English, completed a master's degree, and became certified to teach. In *Young Adult Literature: The Heart of the Middle School Curriculum* (1996), I have told the story of my reintroduction to young adult literature, a story in which my students, as is so often the case, were *my* teachers. I had a young man who was out of context in my 1978 rural Vermont high school; a black-leather kid in an overalls-and-white-socks world, he sat in the back of my room, usually with his head on his desk. One day, to my surprise, he had the textbook open, propped on his desk, and I could see his eyes moving back and forth across the page as the rest of my ninth-grade class and I discussed *Romeo and Juliet*. Ecstatic, I thought, "Yes! Shakespeare is *the* master; he has the power to pull even reluctant readers into his stories!" But then, on his way out the door, Mr. Black Leather threw a slim paperback book at me and yelled, "Hey, teacher, read this!" It turned out he was reading *That Was Then, This Is Now* by S. E. Hinton, under cover of our *Insights* anthology. But, the book literally caught my attention. I took it home, read it in one gulp, and came to class the next day intrigued even more by my student—who came through the door as the bell rang calling, "Did you read it?"

When I answered *yes*, Mr. Black Leather asked how I liked it. I told him it had definitely captured me, that I liked the way the author built the relationship between the main characters, that I was impressed that the author then didn't take the easy way out—that the book ended on a less than happily-ever-after note. My student chimed in with his impressions of the characters, making references to *The Outsiders*, another book by Hinton, and talking—though he didn't use the term—about the theme of the book when he began asking questions about changes and loyalty and doing the right thing. Some other students entered the conversation. Eventually, I got us back to *Romeo and Juliet*, asking about issues of—you guessed it—loyalty and doing the right thing, about parent-child relationships, and about responsibility.

I asked the students if they could suggest other titles that echoed the themes of the play—and of the novel. Several students mentioned *Bridge to Terabithia*. To my delight, they told me it was by my old friend, Katherine Paterson. I asked to borrow a copy; one student brought one to me, and I indulged myself by reading it over the weekend. The next Monday, we had the kinds of literary discussions I'd imagined having with my students as I pursued my English major and teaching credentials—we hit on theme, setting, character, plot; we talked, without really having the names for the theories we were using, from a reader response perspective, from a psychological perspective, from a new critical perspective. My experiences with those ninth graders really set the stage for my development as a believer in the power of young adult literature—literature written about young adults, explicitly for an audience of young adults, and marketed to them—as essential food for young adult readers.

And then, when my daughter, Mandi, was in middle school, my love affair with Katherine Paterson reached a new high. My daughter has one cousin. Born only seven days apart, they are the only grandchildren in the Stover family, and both grandparents doted on them. But my daughter's cousin ended up living with her grandparents, who were in their seventies at the time of the girls' birth, and so were rather set in their ways. Whenever we would visit, Mandi's behavior, food preferences, interests, school achievements, and general way of being in the world were compared, usually unfavorably, to her cousin's. Her grandfather could never understand why she didn't want Frosted Flakes for breakfast, or why she wanted to go to the playground instead of doing crafts. Her grandmother could not seem to remember that she didn't like pink, played soccer, and got up early and went to bed early, and whenever we were anticipating a visit, Mandi was apprehensive, worrying about how her grandparents would compare her this time to her cousin. The girls tended to rub each other the wrong way; holidays usually involved spats of some sort.

I was sad that Mandi and her cousin didn't seem to connect. And then, Mandi was assigned *Jacob Have I Loved*. Her first response was less than enthusiastic because the novel does not have a contemporary setting and she didn't think she wanted to read anything about people in the past. But she "connected" with Louise—Wheeze—she told me, and it hit me that through Wheeze, Mandi was exploring her relationship with her family. Identifying with Wheeze, although an imperfect fit, allowed her to make sense of her place within the family structure and to understand some of her feelings, and to have hope that she could be at peace with the fact that she is not her cousin, and could assert herself with her grandparents without being disrespectful. Although I'd been teaching Paterson's works in my classes for future teachers, and knew *Jacob Have I Loved*, Louise was not a character with whom I felt a great deal of affinity, and I hadn't felt the book's power until I watched my daughter get pulled into a world very different from her own because of the empathy she felt. And as a result of those connections, Mandi was then able to analyze and evaluate the book with a depth of understanding that reminded me, yet again, of the importance of providing young people with books into which they can enter with ease.

The most important experiences leading me to the writing of this book have occurred in my college classes. I have been teaching courses in both children's and young adult literature several times a year every year since

1985. In every course I teach, I try to model for my future teachers how it is possible to have a class of students reading a diverse set of books while coming together for discussion and sharing of responses and analysis through literature circles and other strategies. Thus, for the most part, my students are reading individually selected titles within certain parameters for exploring different genres and other categories of titles I set for them. However, in each class, I require that we all read two books: Cormier's *The Chocolate War* and Paterson's *Bridge to Terabithia*. Additionally, everyone in the class has to read a second work by Paterson. Why? Because Paterson has the ability to make readers enter into the minds and hearts of characters and therefore to experience the world in new ways as a result of connecting to them. Her gift for creating settings that often function almost as characters in her work, her ear for dialogue, her poetic style, and her ability to write eloquently in a number of different genres set her apart from most contemporary writers for young people. While her works have at times been the targets of censors, and while some teachers and parents express concern about the "heaviness" of her topics, her novels are, ultimately, about hope, about love, and about the power, as she says, to find one's way out of the "chaos" from within into "some semblance of order" (1981, 61).

My students have fallen in love, often for the second time, with Paterson titles such as *Bridge to Terabithia* and *Jacob Have I Loved*. They recall with great fondness their first encounters with these books when they were in middle school or high school, and they have wanted to know how to best share Paterson's works with the young people they will be teaching. They have been hungry for ideas about how to ensure parents, guardians, and administrators understand the literary, psychological, and pedagogical value of her books; they have struggled to determine strategies for dealing with her difficult topics in developmentally appropriate ways. They have wanted my recommendations for teaching strategies, for ideas about bridging into Paterson's texts and helping students make connections between their worlds of experience and those of Paterson's characters, and for follow-up activities they can use to ensure their students are responding to the works, and are moving into the kind of critical and creative analysis of them that leads to appreciation for them as works of literary art. As a result of my work with my future teachers, and, the past two summers, with inservice teachers in a graduate course on multicultural literature for children and young adults, I have seen a need for a book that can help all English language arts teachers bring Katherine Paterson's works into their classrooms.

In this book, I focus on several of Paterson's novels for middle and high school readers, as well as her seminal *Bridge to Terabithia*. This Newbery winner is widely taught in fifth grade, which, in many states, is part of the middle school configuration, and it exemplifies so much of what Paterson then explores in her later novels aimed at an older audience. There is a chapter describing the way two middle school teachers use eight different Paterson titles using literature circles, a section on a Guys Night Out discussion of *Come Sing, Jimmy Jo*, and finally a chapter on teaching *Lyddie* and *Jacob Have I Loved* as American historical fiction.

 ## A Note About Context

When I began writing this book, I wanted to serve as a reporter, capturing what excellent teachers of English language arts—those known for their ability to connect even reluctant readers with books—actually did with the books in their classrooms, and what their students had to say in response to the reading. But, caught in another confluence of circumstance, not all the sections of the book have such a significant reality base. The state of Maryland is a part of the Reading First initiative, and, as a result, many school systems have imposed significant restrictions on teachers' abilities to teach novels of their own choosing—and to teach in ways that allow them to open up the world of literature to their students through their own passion and creativity. As new high school assessments and countywide testing have been put into place, teachers' flexibility has become limited; their students have to pass specific exams in order to move to the next grade or to graduate. Their schools have to report adequate yearly progress on the part of all students as part of the No Child Left Behind legislation. In many cases, teachers have been given textbook anthologies that they are told they have to use, with instructions about how to use them, and with admonishments against using precious class time for activities such as read-alouds, silent sustained reading, reading response journals, book talks, grand conversations, and jigsaw groups.

One of my former students managed to incorporate a unit on *Jacob*

Have I Loved into the American literature curriculum but was not permitted by her department chair to use it with honors students due to other curricular mandates. Two middle school teachers were able to squeeze in the use of several Paterson titles toward the end of the year, but only after testing was over. These teachers commented on how grateful they were that their students were engaged in reading sustained narrative, but their comments were poignant and undercut with frustration because of the time limitations. One other middle school teacher was able to use *Come Sing, Jimmy Jo* in his Guys Night Out program, a sort of book club for fathers and sons—no women allowed, not even the school principal, who happened to be female—because this book-based activity was extracurricular, not a part of the regular school day. And yet, all the teachers involved reported that, given the freedom to read with their hearts as well as their minds, students responded to these novels in ways similar to my daughter. And the teachers reported, too, their increased sense of professionalism in being asked to really teach their students using strategies and methods that engaged them in constructing meaning for themselves, in finding personal connections, intertextual connections, and connections between the texts and the outside world.

Thus I write what follows with some sense of sadness that English teachers today have less freedom to meet the needs of their students in some ways than I had when, long ago, my Vermont ninth graders taught me so much about what teaching literature can and should be all about. Nevertheless, the stories of these teachers and their students, and of the bonds they forged as co-sojourners on the literary paths Paterson presents to them, stand as a testament to the power of great authors to help readers—of all ages—transcend the limits reality often otherwise imposes as they learn about themselves, each other, and the world through reading.

Bridge to Terabithia and Its Bridges to the Young

Teaching a "Difficult" Text

Summary: When Jess is beaten by Leslie Burke, a girl, in his quest to be the fastest runner in fifth grade, a new chapter in his life begins as he and Leslie create the magical kingdom of Terabithia. After tragedy strikes, Jess passes along all that he has learned from Leslie in order to honor her memory and to maintain the sense of self she helped him achieve.

Quintessential Paterson

In our conversations about teaching the novels of Katherine Paterson, the teachers with whom I collaborated on this project remarked several times that if they were to work with Paterson's books again in the future, they would do much more homework. Three of the four teachers spent considerable time researching the author's life and times as a backdrop for helping their students better understand her characters and her themes, and they found themselves eager to know anything I could tell them about her own experiences as a child, young adult, mother, and writer. All of the teachers noted that they did not always feel such a need to know the authors they teach, but with Paterson, the biographical information opened up her works and created connections among them and between the works and their students' experiences in ways they found valuable (personal conversations with Betsy Gardiner, Mary Christensen, Kathy Slingland.)

In the interest of space, a biographical summary of Paterson's life is not included in this text. There is, however, a lengthy biography available on *www.heinemann.com* ("Who Is Katherine Paterson?"), and Gary Schmidt's (1994) *Presenting Katherine Paterson* is a book-length critical biography that is rich in detail and analysis of her works. It is important, however, for readers of *Bridge to Terabithia* to know that Paterson wrote this story after her son's best friend, a young girl, was struck and killed by lightning when they were in third grade. To those critics who do not believe children so young should be exposed to such tragedy in their reading, Paterson replies, "I can not, will not, withhold from my young readers the harsh realities of human hunger and suffering and loss, but neither will I neglect to plant that stubborn seed of hope that has enabled our race to outlast wars and famines and the desecration of death" (1981, 139).

Bridge to Terabithia: Paterson's Core Value

Understanding *Bridge to Terabithia* is crucial in developing an under-standing of the themes and issues Paterson explores in the body of her work, and in helping to articulate the relationship, for Paterson, between love, friendship, being an outsider, hope, and grace. This chapter also examines some of the key biographical elements of Paterson's life as they intertwine with her fiction. As timely now as it was when Paterson wrote it in 1977, *Bridge to Terabithia* demonstrates for young readers what it means to take the risks involved in forming bonds of friendship across gender lines, in learning to love and lose a loved one, and in finding ways to share the secrets of these insights with others. Middle school students, through reading it, can explore, as my future teachers do, the relevance of these topics for themselves as they come of age in a world in which transience and uncertainty is a way of life for so many of us.

When my daughter was in fifth grade, her teacher saved *Bridge to*

Terabithia to use as a read-aloud at the end of the school year. But in spite of the fact that Jess and Leslie entered into the lives of these students about three weeks before summer vacation, the reality of band concerts, field trips, county testing days, and an outbreak of lice meant that, on the last day of school, there were still several chapters yet to go. Mandi has always been a "take the world as it comes" sort of child, and she did not seem to mind the lack of closure but I wanted her to feel Paterson's compelling description of forgiveness and grace that comes at the novel's end. So, I got out my copy of the book and we put aside the novel we were in the midst of reading at night before bed, and we finished the story of *Bridge* on our own. I had trouble reading on that summer evening when we were approaching the last page; the tears in my eyes that always form when I envision Jess and May Belle entering the Kingdom of Terabithia clouded my vision, and Mandi asked why I was crying, wanting to know if someone else were about to die. "No," I croaked, and continued on, until Mandi pulled the book from my hands and took over. When she came to the last word, she closed the novel, pulled me into a hug, and said, "Now I know why you said I had to finish the book." We did not say much else; we just sat there in the quiet, listening to the spring peepers and watching fireflies flit across the darkening sky, sharing the experience of being uplifted and changed, at least in some small way, by understanding, through Jess, more deeply the meaning of grace, and by having, through him, a model of what it means to live in the world in a way that honors the lessons Leslie had to teach.

In spite of the incredible loss Jess has experienced, both he and his readers *know* that Leslie has taught him about hope and love, and these are lessons we know he is now poised to share himself, as he invites May Belle into the magical kingdom of Terabithia. "And it is that hope, rooted not merely in sheer blind optimism but in a real understanding that the world can be a difficult and bitter place, which enables Paterson's characters not only to keep going but in some measure triumph over circumstances. . . . The pain is still there, and the hardship is not minimized, but there is hope for a better life" (Schmidt, 1994, 444).

I usually end the sequence of classes in my Children's and Young Adult Literature class that we spend on *Bridge* by reading Paterson's own words about the book from her Newbery acceptance speech, and I almost always find myself crying in front of my students just as I did when reading with Mandi. Paterson notes that children often do not like the ending of the novel; they rebel against the notion that Jess would share his and Leslie's magical kingdom with his younger sister—and the hint that the thumbsucking Joyce Ann may eventually be allowed to enter Terabithia as well. Paterson says she listens to them but does not argue with them, for

> I know as well as they do that May Belle is not Leslie, nor will she ever be. But perhaps someday they will understand Jess's bridge as an act of grace, which he built not because of who May Belle was, but because of who he himself had become crossing the gully into Terabithia. I allowed him to build the bridge because I dare to believe . . . that the very valley where evil and despair defeat us can become a gate of hope—if there is a bridge. (1981, 114–15)

Bridge is a novel that many of my future teachers know. Their teachers or family members read this novel to them, or they read it on their own or as part of a class unit of study. They have grown up with this powerful story about the friendship between Jess Aarons and Leslie Burke as both readers and viewers of the movie version. They want to share its power with their own students, and yet are afraid of teaching the book precisely because it is so powerful and because it deals with topics, including death, with which they are not comfortable. So one of my goals in using *Bridge* in my class is to model strategies that these future teachers can feel confident using in their own classrooms.

Introducing the Novel

I introduce the novel on the second day of the semester by doing a structured web activity on the word *bridge* (this is an activity we repeat in a slightly different form later in the semester when we talk about the concept of bridging into literature in general). In groups, students are asked to put the word *bridge* in the middle of a circle on a piece of newsprint. They draw spokes out from the circle with the terms *kinds of bridges, reasons for bridges,* and *synonyms for bridge* at the ends. Each student has a marker and they begin adding information to the web, playing off of each other as they do so.

They usually start by listing kinds of bridges; they seem to come to mind quickly because they are tangible and everyone has experience with various kinds of bridges: covered, suspension, railroad, tunnels, plank, rope, swinging, drawbridges, and so on. Eventually someone gets a bit silly and says "bridge of my nose." From there, students begin to include other less obvious kinds of bridges—those on a string instrument, dental bridges, the game of bridge. I prompt them to look at their list and generalize about *why* we have bridges; again, they start with the obvious reasons: to shorten distances, to connect two points, to make travel easier. Then they push a bit further: to make travel safer, to open up the world and make otherwise inaccessible places accessible, to provide support, to enhance an experience (in music), to form what are sometimes unlikely friendships (the game of bridge). Synonyms take the longest to generate, probably because they are less concrete, but we end up with lists of verbs, mostly: to connect, to support, to close gaps.

Following this activity, we post our webs on the wall and leave them there until we get to the point in the semester when we actually discuss Paterson's novel. I then ask them to freewrite about one of two things:

- An imaginary world they created as children, telling them about my own neighborhood collaboration to turn my family's patio into the spaceship from the very old and well-forgotten show *Lost in Space,* where we would then enact our own adventures similar to those of the crew from those episodes.

- An unlikely friendship they either formed themselves and why that happened, or an unlikely friendship they witnessed in some way.

I give them about three minutes to write, and then we move into groups again. Students find at least two other class members who wrote about the same topic. They share their responses and their group task, posted on the board, is to arrive at generalizations about either the nature of and reasons for creating imaginary worlds or the nature of and reasons for unlikely friendships. Group recorders collect these generalizations on more sheets of newsprint, present them to the larger group, and we conclude by coming up with three to five generalizations for each topic. My classes usually include a mix of men and women, some traditional undergraduates, some returning older students. In the past, classes have arrived at the following statements:

> Imaginary worlds are places of escape. They allow us to practice using our imaginations. They are often lovely places that represent what we want the world to be like. But they often mirror our everyday world with its negative features too and so when we go into them we can practice figuring out how to deal with those bad parts in a safe place.

> Unlikely friendships occur between boys and girls, between older and younger people, between people with disabilities and those who are not disabled, between people and pets or animals, between people of different faiths or world views, between people from countries where the governments are not friendly. These friendships happen because, in spite of difference, the individuals involved find points of connection. Sometimes it's symbiotic, too; the "friends" can help each other because they are so different.

My students often note that, as a class, they make friends of all ages because the older class members know a lot, have a lot of life experience, and are emotionally stable, while the younger class participants share their enthusiasm, idealism, and energy.

Now that we have considered the concepts of *bridge, imaginary worlds,* and *unlikely friendships* in the abstract, I hold up *Bridge to Terabithia,* ask how many have read it, tell them it always makes me cry, and show them on the syllabus the date by which they need to have read it. I point out that the syllabus gives them instructions for posting an email to me by 8:00 A.M. of the morning of that date that includes the following information:

- a summary of the novel in no more than three sentences

- a paragraph about whether the unlikely friendship between Jess and Leslie and their magical kingdom reflect our generalizations from our discussion

- a paragraph about the different kinds of bridges that exist in the book and how our work on the concept of bridge relates to the themes of Paterson's work

My students leave the class having experienced a bridge into the novel that provides a scaffold for their reading and gives me a starting point for launching into the six hours of class time we spend on this novel.

Note that in this course, I also try to model for my future teachers the variety of strategies at their disposal for using a novel with an entire class of students. We talk about the pros and cons of having an entire book due on a particular date, of assigning sections of the book one day at a time, or of assigning larger chunks of the book to be read by several different dates spanning across two or three weeks, so that in class the teacher deals with section one for several days, while the students are reading at home to complete the next section. We talk about reading aloud, using books on tape, showing the movie version—and whether to show it before the book is read, while the book is being read, or after the book has been read. For my unit on *Bridge,* I know from experience that most readers, once they start it, read it through in one big gulp, which is why I assign the whole text to be completed by a specific date. There is a made-for-television movie of *Bridge,* and a new Hollywood version, and I offer students extra credit to watch the film on their own and participate in a discussion forum about it.

In-Class Activities

On the day everyone is to come to class having read the novel, the first thing students have to do upon entering the room is to write their brief summary of the plot on the board. I'm fortunate to teach in a long, skinny room with a blackboard across the entire front and a white board lining one whole side. Even in a class of thirty-two students, there's space for everyone to write. In a different kind of space, I have asked students to use markers to write out their summaries on construction paper and to stick the sheets on the walls with masking tape. Then we all move about the room, trying to find the key elements of the book, those to which almost everyone alludes in their summaries. In the past, we have arrived at the following commonalities: Jess and Leslie's friendship, fifth grade, rural Virginia, overcoming fears, Terabithia, Leslie's death, and lessons learned by Jess. I ask these students, primarily future teachers, the value of this activity for younger readers. They tell me that they like the activity because summarizing is hard, and this way, they can tell if everyone understood the basics of the book. They also note that seeing what others have written helps them recognize aspects of the novel they may not have included; for instance, if someone has left out setting, seeing that setting is mentioned numerous times helps the student begin to think more about that element of the story and why it is so important to the plot. The activity gives me, as the instructor, a sense of our common ground, which is crucial to being able to plunge into the next round of activities. I have used all these activities in various forms and in diverse orders. Because everybody has read the whole book by the time we begin our work in class, I can adjust the sequence of activities based on what themes or issues emerge as we engage in any particular event.

Creative Dramatics: Tableaux

In the case of my children's and young adult literature classes, because the theme of *overcoming fears* shows up in the majority of the summaries, I often decide to use a creative dramatics technique to investigate the various plot threads Paterson weaves together in order to create a richly textured exploration of this theme. I ask the students to break into groups of five. I tell them they've been charged with creating exhibits for the new Wax Museum of Children's and Young Adult Literature. They are to generate several different tableaux that could be used to document how Paterson addresses the theme of overcoming fears; I tell them that other, fictional, classes will be asked to come up with tableaux about how other authors deal with this theme. Each group has to brainstorm a list of characters and situations in which they have to confront their fears. Then they each have to model for us two possible exhibits—tableaux/frozen statues—they feel are central to the novel. We don't talk about what *central* means until after each group presents its exhibit. They are free to use anything in the room as props, but they have only ten minutes to make their decision, practice, and get ready to show the rest of the class. Each group has to choose a student who will act as their curator. This individual will first ask the larger class to guess what scene is being portrayed and then will describe what we are seeing, tell us who the characters are, what they are doing, what fear is being overcome, and why this scene is central to the novel.

Almost every group in any class in which I teach this novel chooses to illustrate the scene from the end of the novel in which Jess saves May Belle from falling into the creek. Up until this point, Jess has been afraid of the water when it gets high and, at least in part, he chose to go with Miss Edmunds to the museums of DC rather than go with Leslie to fight the evil she said was facing Terabithia because he was fearful of the rushing waters. But groups then vary widely on their other choices, which range from portraying Janice crying after learning her two friends have told the rest of the school community that her father beats her; to Leslie being teased at the beginning of the school year by other girls and Jess' reaction; to Jess being criticized by his father; to Jess standing up to Janice on the bus and Jess writing about football as his favorite hobby when he really hates it; to Jess responding when Leslie reads her essay about scuba diving and panics; and finally to Jess' mother in a bad temper at the beginning of the book. As each group takes a turn freezing into its tableaux and the curators make their comments, the audience members are charged with, again, making generalizations about what causes each individual's fear and what the individual does—or could do—to overcome it. The list of fears is wide ranging. Some characters fear not being accepted by others, which puts Janice and Jess into the same category. Some characters fear things outside their control—Jess' mother is afraid of having too little money and Jess is afraid of the creek. Some characters fear not being able to take care of those they love—Jess' mother and Leslie connect on this point. Some characters fear lack of love—Jess and May Belle share this trait.

With other groups of students, I've asked students to focus their attention on specific aspects of the book. Sometimes I've asked them to portray a decision-making point, a point at which either a character—or Paterson—could have made a different decision that would have taken the story line in a different direction. In other groups, I've talked about Paterson's belief in the importance of creative problem solving and have asked the groups to portray a point at which a character solves a problem in a creative way. One incident that almost always is selected when I focus the tableaux in this manner is the scene in which May Belle wants to beat up Janice for having stolen her Twinkies. Jess and Leslie talk her out of this violent option and then decide to make Janice look foolish instead. After seeing tableaux that illustrate these points in the story, we can discuss how we all would do well to be creative in the face of violence, striving for nonviolent solutions to difficult situations. With future teachers, I compare May Belle's reaction to those of Jess and Leslie from a developmental psychology perspective, asking what it is we know from theorists such as Piaget or Kohlberg or Gilligan that might explain the difference in their responses to Janice Avery.

Categorizing Characters

The discussion of how characters are similar, sometimes, in their fears, leads to another discussion strategy. I ask students to work with a partner to generate a list of categories into which they could group individuals from Paterson's world. Obviously, we have boys and girls. We have the groupings that emerged from discussion of fears. Other groupings from this class included: givers and takers; those who care for others and those who don't; artists and nonartists; adults and children; bullies and those bullied; leaders and followers. As we list these headings on the board and begin to see who might go under each heading, we find unexpected parallels. Janice and Leslie were placed in both categories— bullies and bullied—which led us to discuss the role of Janice in the book in general and why Paterson introduced her into a story essentially about Jess and Leslie.

When I ask my classes why so many groups choose, for their tableaux, a scene from the end of the novel, either that in which Jess saves May Belle or that in which he builds a bridge to Terabithia for her, we get into a discussion of the fact that this novel belongs to Jess. It is about how Leslie's presence in his life forever changes him, giving him strength to confront his own very real and less tangible fears, and to grow in understanding and sophistication and self-knowledge as a result. Without taking the actions he takes in these scenes, he would not, as one of my students noted, be able to "pay back to the world in beauty and caring what Leslie had loaned to him in vision and strength" (Paterson 1987, 126). Jess definitely falls into the category of givers but, surprisingly, so does May Belle, who gives of herself to her brother when she follows him to Terabithia, despite his hitting her in the face, because she doesn't want him to be lonesome.

Building Bridges

At this point in the class, we revisit our initial posters about bridges. I ask, "What kinds of bridges does Paterson create in *Bridge*?" Students talk, of course, about the literal bridge to Terabithia. But they also talk about how characters, through their actions, build bridges between and among themselves. Jess helps Mr. Burke fix up the old farm, thus building a bridge between himself and a man he had previously compared to a canker sore. Jess' art is a bridge between himself and Miss Edmunds. Leslie's research into and caring for endangered animals is something Jess turns into a bridge Leslie can cross in order to connect with Janice Avery.

Guided Listening

It's at this point that I can introduce some of Paterson's biographical history, asking students how having this knowledge better bridges any gaps that exist for them as readers. We talk about the concept of the teacher as the bridge—teachers, as more sophisticated readers with more knowledge of resources and more experience in exploring texts using multiple theoretical approaches, can provide information about the author's life, about the historical context in which a work was written, about whether the cultural norms and language usage of the time are reflected in a work, about what critics have said about a work, or about their own personal experiences with other works by the same author.

Reading *Bridge* provides a great opportunity for middle school readers to begin to understand the ways in which an author's life influences his or her work. I've used a Guided Listening activity to provide practice with close listening. Students receive a copy of the reading with blanks where I have underlined words. They listen for me to fill in the blanks as I talk through a brief biographical overview of Paterson's life and work. (Note that samples of these handouts for this activity—PTM 1 and PTM 2—and other teaching materials mentioned in the text are available on *www.heinemann.com* [see Paterson Teaching Materials].) After hearing about Paterson's early history, about how she came to write *Bridge*, and something about her beliefs about writing and reading, students work in pairs to complete the following activity:

1. First, make a Venn diagram comparing Paterson to Jess and Leslie. Points of comparison that have been made include
   - They are outsiders (Paterson was "foreign").
   - She liked to read and write and a librarian helped her find solace the way a teacher helped Jess.
   - She believes in the power of imagination, creating the novel *Bridge*, as Leslie creates Terabithia.
   - She and Jess know rural Virginia.
   - She is missionary and Christian like Jess.
   - They both have persistence—Paterson as a writer and Jess with his running.
   - They both experienced losing someone special.
   - Jess provides a bridge to May Belle as Paterson provides a bridge into the scary world in which death happens but can be survived by writing the book.

2. Now decide: Is *Bridge* about the time when Paterson didn't receive any valentines at school?

Making the Abstract Concrete: Introducing Symbolism
Another activity I've done in my course that can easily be transferred to the middle school classroom is one that involves thinking symbolically—but in a concrete way. Middle school students are, for the most part, solidly ensconced in Piaget's "concrete operational stage" of thinking and most students can, with support and Vygotskian scaffolding,

begin to think more abstractly; thus this is a perfect time for introducing the concept of *symbolism* (Woolfolk 2004, 14–55).

Objects in a Bag. Students work in groups of five to determine a list of ten items they can both find and then fit into a brown paper grocery bag. These ten items have to be symbolic or representative of ten key events in the story that take the reader from the opening page to its close. They write out rationales for their choices during class. It works well to hand out ten index cards and have each student take responsibility for writing about two objects. Each student signs his or her name and the group members initial each card to indicate their agreement. Their homework is to divide responsibility for collecting the items on their list so that, after the first five minutes of class the next day, they have all ten objects in a bag, which I provide. The warm-up activity for this second day of class is to draw one item on the outside of the bag that they feel is *the* most important object—it can be an item they have placed inside the bag or it can be something they could not actually find or create.

Once the groups have finished drawing their picture and putting their objects in their bag, I collect the bags and redistribute them to other groups. Members of the groups take turns pulling objects out of the bags and describing to their peers why they believe the object was included. Everybody helps to craft a rationale for the object, but each group member again takes responsibility for writing two rationales on new index cards, which they initial. I usually use white cards for the original rationales and colored cards for the second set.

The bags are then returned to their original groups. Students get the index cards they originally wrote as well as the cards from the group that had their bag. Then I ask the groups to write out at least three reasons why they chose the picture they drew on the front of their bags. At this point, someone from each group serves as spokesperson. To try to ensure students all have the opportunity to practice public speaking at some point, I vary the strategy I use to select a spokesperson: I might ask the person whose birthday is closest to the day we're in class to do this; or I might ask the person who brought in the object that represents the first significant element in the book to serve; or I might ask the person who has the fewest cousins to report. We hear from all the groups and then, individually, students are assigned homework based on the day's events:

Convince Me: Imagine that you have been asked to come up with a logo for the new *Bridge to Terabithia* movie. The producer wants a crisp, clean visual image, just one object, to put on the initial advertising posters. The name of the book will also appear, either under or over or through the image. You must choose the image from the pictures drawn on the front of the bags and come to class prepared to argue for that particular image. Write a paragraph in which you tell me, the producer, the object, its significance within the book on a literal level (who actually uses it or comes into contact with it), its significance within the book on the thematic level (how the object is more important than just its literal use), and the three reasons why you believe this object would be the most effective visual aspect of the logo.

Make Ice Cream: Paterson says that revising is a way of turning spilled milk into ice cream (Sanderson 2004, 56). Take the index cards you wrote about the two items you contributed to your group's bag of objects, and compare what you said to what was said by the member of the group who received your bag. Write me, again as the producer of the movie version of *Bridge*, a paragraph convincing me that, no matter what, I have to fund the purchase of these items to be part of the set. Use your reasons as well as any insights you received from the other writer. If you decide to quote directly from what the other writer had to say, somehow indicate that you are citing his or her words by using quotation marks and a citation, for example (Smith, in class July 7, 2005).

When we return to class the next day, I ask for a vote from the Convince Me activity to determine which image the class believes is the best one for the advertising project. I'm always amazed at the diversity of responses. While the rope Leslie and Jess use to cross the creek is almost always one of the options, other items routinely appear on the bags and win votes: a crown, a paintbrush, the funeral wreath, a castle, the woods, and Prince Terrien.

Objects in a Bag Variation #1. Another way to work with objects in a bag is to assign each group a different character from the book: Leslie, Jess,

Miss Edmunds, Jess' father, Jess' mother, May Belle, Mr. Burke, and Janice Avery all work well. Each group has to find either pictures or actual objects that somehow reflect or symbolize the character and his or her character traits, which they put into a small bag. They swap bags with another group and have to guess which character is being represented and then indicate whether they would keep all the objects originally chosen or would make substitutions.

Objects in a Bag Variation #2. A third way to work with objects in a bag is for the teacher to bring in a bag that includes pictures and objects reflective of important people, events, and themes in the book. I sometimes reach into the bag and randomly select an item, then toss it to someone in the room who has to tell the rest of us its significance. That person then selects an object or picture and gives it to someone else in the class; we keep going until everyone has had a chance to explain an object—the last student to choose an item passes the bag back to me and I pull out and explain the final object. A can of beans, a picture of a cow, a photo of a school playground, a wreath of flowers, a photo of a girl sucking her thumb, a scuba mask, a picture of a school bathroom, a friendship knot, a CD or tape labeled *Free to Be You and Me*, an Easter basket, images of DC or postcards from the Smithsonian, a picture of a shovel, a picture of a farm, a dollar bill, a Christmas tree photo, a love letter signed Willard Hughes, a model or toy television set—these are all items I've included in my bag of goodies. If I have a large class and don't have enough objects for each student, I have students explain in pairs.

Collages. Similar to the Object in a Bag activities, making collages can be a useful way to help younger readers begin to think symbolically. Groups work with large pieces of newsprint and magic markers by folding the newsprint or chart paper in three columns or rows. They brainstorm three themes or issues they believe Paterson is consciously exploring in *Bridge,* and then they work to represent these themes with images (no words) from magazines. Groups hang their posters on the walls and we do a gallery walk, trying to identify the themes that the groups are reflecting with their collages. Themes that have been identified include outsiders/insiders, jealousy, friendship, dealing with loss, being true to oneself, and the importance of connection.

Another option for collages is to ask groups, or individuals, to divide their papers in half; on one side of the collage they represent *reality*, and on the other side, they represent *the ideal*, from a specific character's point of view. Students have to be able to defend their choices based on the text by citing page numbers at the bottom of each side of the paper. It is easy for younger readers to portray the difference between the reality of Jess' life or Leslie's life and the ideal setting of Terabithia, but they can make interesting inferences when asked to depict the real versus the ideal for other characters—what does Janice Avery want in her ideal world? Miss Edmunds? Jess' father?

Interdisciplinary Connections

In addition to being rich with all the features that make this novel a delicious read, both for individuals and for group discussion, Paterson's book is also rich in references that allow the creative teacher to lead students into consideration of topics and issues important to other disciplines. I end my discussion of *Bridge* in my course for future teachers by brainstorming interdisciplinary connections that middle school students might research, so that they can then practice the skills required when reading to be informed while we're practicing reading for aesthetic purposes in going through the novel. A small sampling of the topics we have listed includes Jacques Cousteau, killer whales, timber wolves, redwoods, the Smithsonian and other DC museums, research on the effect of television viewing on children, regulations regarding a teacher's ability to transport a student, and bullies.

Hurray for Teachers

Bridge to Terabithia is a powerful reminder of the need for teachers to reach out to the Jess and Leslies of the world. Paterson remarks, in her

Newbery acceptance speech, that she uses the word *banzai* on the dedication page of her novel because she wants to honor teachers:

> It is a cry of triumph and joy, a word full of hope in the midst of the world's contradictory evidence. It is the word I wanted to say through *Bridge to Terabithia*. It is a word I think Leslie Burke would have liked. It is my salute to all of you whose lives are bridges for the young. (1981, 115)

Katherine Paterson Literature Circles Project

 Introducing Mary and Kathy

Mary Christensen and Kathy Slingland teach English language arts at Esperanza Middle School, one of three middle schools that are part of St. Mary's County Public Schools, located in St. Mary's County, MD. When I first met with Mary and Kathy, they were excited about the possibility of having their students read whole novels written by someone whose literary skill and evocative language are exceptionally able to draw middle school students into the world of her texts. We brainstormed possible titles that might be a good fit with the literature curriculum followed by the St. Mary's County Public Schools, but by the time the project was ready to be implemented, the county had changed its textbook series and, as a voluntary participant in the Reading First network, no longer allowed individual teachers to make choices about which titles to use in the classroom, nor about strategies to employ when teaching selections from the textbook series.

Mary and Kathy were disheartened but determined to find some way to participate in my project, both because of their own love of Katherine Paterson's work, and because of their convictions about the importance of empowering middle school students as readers.

After much discussion, Mary and Kathy decided to use the Paterson project as a way to introduce their students to the concept of literature circles, and to help them better understand how an author's life experiences can influence his or her choice of theme and the ways those themes play out in his or her work. Literature circles involve placing small groups of students together for in-depth discussion of a text they have all read; their discussions usually begin as students share their personal responses to the book, and then they collaborate to construct a deeper understanding of it as they ask each other questions, and work to clarify their understanding of how the piece of literature works and why it evoked the responses in them that it did. The teacher facilitates the discussion but the students own it, and typically, each small group of students has read a different text (Daniels 2002; Schlick Noe and Johnson 1999).

Kathy employed one cycle of literature circles complemented by higher-order thinking enrichment activities. Mary followed two cycles of literature circles with a culminating project. In general, Kathy's students were in a homogenous class for students whose academic performance and reading skills put them ahead of their peers. Mary's classes were heterogeneously grouped and included a number of students with special needs, including documented learning disabilities, attention deficit hyperactivity disorder (ADHD), and other medical and emotional difficulties.

Summaries

Given the personalities, interests, and reading abilities of their students, ranging from three and four years below grade level to a high of eleventh and twelfth grade, Mary and Kathy selected the following titles:

Bridge to Terabithia: See Chapter 2.

The Field of the Dogs: Josh thinks the world is just so unfair. He's had to move to Vermont, he's now got a squawking baby brother and a new stepfather. And he's got to face a bully at his new school, just as his dog has to face a threatening opponent.

The Great Gilly Hopkins: After years in the foster care system, Gilly has developed quite an attitude. Maime Trotter, her new foster mother, sees beneath Gilly's hard exterior and helps her satisfy her need for love and self-acceptance.

Jacob Have I Loved: Growing up on isolated Rass Island during World War II, Louise is bitter that her younger twin, more beautiful and talented, though fragile, seems to get everything she wants and needs, while "Wheeze" has to fend for herself. This story of sibling rivalry ends in reconciliation once Louise comes to understand her family, herself, and her own hidden talents.

Park's Quest: Park is on a quest, like the knights of old. But Park's in search of his father, and in the process of finding out about his dad, he learns many surprising things about his family and himself.

Preacher's Boy: As the twentieth century dawns, many members of the congregation at Robbie's father's church believe the world is about to end. Set at this historical moment, the novel chronicles Robbie's search for connection and friendship.

The Sign of the Chrysanthemum: In this adventure novel of samurais and medieval Japan, Muna, whose name means *No Name,* goes in search of both his father and his own sense of identity.

 ## Logistics for the Project

Kathy and Mary each provided "book blessings" for the eight titles; the teachers gave brief, inviting overviews of the books, telling what they most appreciated about them as readers themselves. After hearing about each of the options, students listed their top four choices and were told that they would be assigned to read one of those four. Then each teacher put students into groups based on the selections; groups consisted of no more than five and no fewer than three readers. These groups were titled literature discussion circles. Each group determined how many pages its members would read on a daily basis during the two weeks in which literature circles took place using a group planning sheet. (See samples of Mary and Kathy's handouts on *www.heinemann.com*: PTM 3, PTM 4,

PTM 5, and PTM 6.) The students had two weeks—ten class sessions and the intervening weekend—to read their novel and complete their literature circle responsibilities, and then they had another week to complete book-related projects, such as journal entries and logs (see PTM 7 and 8, and student samples PTM 9 and 10).

Additionally, each group member received literature discussion preparation sheets to complete after each daily reading session (see PTM 11 and 12, and student sample PTM 13). The objective for providing these reading forms was to aid students in recalling information, responding to their chosen selection, and thinking about their book in preparation for their participation in their literature circles. These preparation sheets were graded strictly on whether they were completed.

The literature circle groups held discussions each day. The teachers circulated the room, visiting two to three groups per class session during the twenty to twenty-five minutes of class time devoted to the project. Kathy and Mary completed observation assessments as they circulated as a way to assist them in providing feedback to the groups about their progress in discussion skill, and as a way to keep track of student participation. After literature circle time, students again read on their own—any chunk of reading not completed in class that was due to be discussed the next class session was homework.

At the completion of the literature circle cycle, students worked on higher-order thinking activities. They also completed brief constructed response (BCRs) items, which mirrored the kind of BCRs they would encounter on state and county reading assessments. Most of these BCRs asked students to work on thematic issues. Students also answered questions related to the impact of Paterson's life on her work, compared two works, and completed extension projects of their own choosing.

 ## Practicing for Paterson

Because of recent changes in the St. Mary's County reading curriculum, Kathy and Mary knew that their students would not have developed the specific skills required for successful participation in literature circles. As they wrote in their journal for the project, they "had to introduce, model, use student exemplars, and have students practice doing literature circles" before they could plunge into a literature circle-based approach to Paterson. The teachers used Harvey Daniels' (2002) *Literature Circles: Voice and Choice in Book Clubs and Reading Groups* as their guide in developing activities designed to foster students' understanding of their responsibilities within literature circles. They practiced the literature circle concept using two short stories from the anthologies they were assigned to use as textbooks.

Mary and Kathy also wanted students to know something of Paterson's biography prior to reading their chosen novel not only because they believe that establishing such background knowledge is crucial to understanding Paterson's themes and characters but because they could engage students in guided listening and notetaking activities, which are essential reading skills to have when reading for information.

Mary and Kathy downloaded a biographical sketch of Paterson by Eric Peterson from the Internet. Because of their students' differing reading ability and levels of reading sophistication, the teachers read this biography to the students, pausing to ask questions and encourage predicting, and following the reading with discussion and question-and-answer periods. As they worked through the project, they also found those references preceded by an asterisk in this book's Works Cited section particularly useful.

During Reading

In general, during their independent reading of each chunk of the text that their reading groups determined were to be read for each class session, students completed reading guides. The guides included space in which students summarized what they read, outlined connections they could make between the reading and information at their disposal on Paterson's life, completed reader response starters, attended to new or important vocabulary terms, and responded to "What If and Why?" or other higher-order thinking questions (PTM 11 and 12 and student sample PTM 9 on *www.heinemann.com*). Students had to come to their literature circle with a completed sheet in order to participate in the discussion.

Because vocabulary is often a stumbling block to readers, but because these teachers recognize that by middle school students often have different vocabulary needs, students were also responsible for noting words that they found either problematic as they tried to make sense of a passage, or words that intrigued them because of their sound or usage. They kept track of these words on their reading response sheets, and at the end of the book, they had to select just ten words that they wanted to own for themselves. Then, in order to help students store these words in their memories, they used word art, bubble letters, or any other artistic technique to present the word on the page in a way that somehow conveys its meaning. They also produced the more traditional definition and sentence using the word accurately. Their final products illustrate the power of individual choice in even such a routine component of English teaching as vocabulary development. Figure 3–1 is just one among many student samples that shows the value of the visual component, something Kylene Beers (2006) has been researching of late.

Several student response sheets are also included on *www .heinemann.com* (see student sample PTMs 14, 15, 16, and 17). What is intriguing is how the students zero in on aspects of the text that might never receive attention if the teacher is always responsible for asking questions. Given the invitation to respond to the text in open-ended ways, while also being provided with a structure for thinking about their reactions, these middle school students ask questions of the author and express opinions about sections of text that demonstrate they are reading closely, and with an eye toward detail—both in order to better comprehend the story line but also to support their developing evaluative skills. Sarah, writing about a section of *Jacob* in which Louise tries to say she is not "cussing," likes how Paterson has Louise say "Cussing is like 'God' and 'hell' and 'damn'" (67) because it shows "how Louise is smart and bull-headed because she is able, in this sentence, to use cuss words in a legal sort of way." But Sarah does not like that the Captain has illegal wine. She does not think this fits his character, and this becomes an issue she wants to talk through with her literature circle.

Ruth, like Sarah, often questions decisions that Paterson makes. At

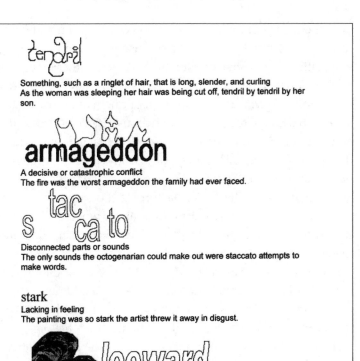

tendril
Something, such as a ringlet of hair, that is long, slender, and curling
As the woman was sleeping her hair was being cut off, tendril by tendril by her son.

armageddon
A decisive or catastrophic conflict
The fire was the worst armageddon the family had ever faced.

staccato
Disconnected parts or sounds
The only sounds the octogenarian could make out were staccato attempts to make words.

stark
Lacking in feeling
The painting was so stark the artist threw it away in disgust.

leeward
On or toward the side to which the wind is blowing
The leeward house was quickly destroyed during the storm.

FIGURE 3–1 *Sarah's vocabulary art assignment*

one point, in writing about *Park's Quest*, she says, "Why didn't Park ever look through the books [of his father] before?" She is not sure she believes that he would not have stumbled across them earlier in his life. But, she does find much of the book believable because Paterson's details about what people do in daily life echo with her own experience; she can picture in her mind Park and his mom reading together because of her own memories of reading stories together with her mother. She is also very curious about why Paterson wrote this novel. Almost every day, Ruth wants to ask her reading group, "Why did Katherine write this book? Did she experience someone dying when she was little?"

What teacher would have predicted that Dillon would identify with Muna, from *The Sign of the Chrysanthemum*, when Muna is confused and overwhelmed because he is not religious and so cannot identify temples or religions symbols (1988, 100) because Dillon, too, has felt confused when attending a different church? And yet, at other times, Dillon cannot condone Muna's actions; he can say, "I know Muna was mad at Fukuji for not giving him an answer, but he had no reason to steal his sword." But Dillon recognizes that he must not be understanding Muna and so brings to his group the question, "What *did* cause Muna to steal the sword from Fukuji?" However, Joseph does not have any problem understanding why Muna has stolen the sword; instead, he wants the group to discuss, "Why did Muna burry [sic] the sword?"

And students, prompted to think about whether their books connected to any other titles in their experience in an open-ended way, made interesting comparisons. One student said of *Sign*, "This is a lot like a story I once read called 'The Hand' where this dark sorcerer has a hand that brings incredible power to its owner. Other people became jealous and one day a young boy steals the hand and then the power is too much for him so he returns it and notices that the sorcerer isn't dark, really." Another student responded by saying he could see that connection, but thought Muna was more like Stanley in "the book *Holes* because of how Zero and Stanley and Muna all run away and they have these adventures on their own and have to figure out a lot of stuff on their own and grow up in the process."

After Reading

After reading the entire book, students had several activities on which to work. With the groups as a whole, Kathy and Mary revisited the biographical selection and had a more in-depth discussion of the relationship between Paterson's own lived experiences and those of her characters. As Mary writes, "There were many 'a-has' this time around as students really saw the connections between their books and Paterson's life." One student called out, "Her books are pieces of her life!"

All the students involved in the project completed the same two brief constructed response writings. One focused on theme; one focused on biography-to-text connections. In Mary's classes, students then completed a diary entry, a Sketch-to-Stretch about a favorite character, and wrote a book review. In Kathy's classes, students created and presented PowerPoint book talks in their literature circle groups. Both teachers attended to state curricular outcomes in creating these activities; each teacher wanted students to practice writing in different genres and for different audiences. Then, while Kathy's classes continued working on higher-order thinking activities, such as a one-pager, a Mandala, a character cinquain, and a story pyramid (reproducibles available on *www.heinemann.com*: PTM 18, 19, 20, 21, and 22), Mary's classes began a second round of literature circles.

These activities promote the development of students' abilities to summarize—articulating the heart of the plot tensions, a character's personality, or an author's theme— without being asked to "summarize." It seems to be the combinations of the tensions of structure and choice, and writing and design that prompt insights into the gestalts of the texts for students who, according to their teachers, sometimes struggle when asked for such thinking.

Before they do their one-pager, students think about themes by completing one of two worksheets (PTM 23 and 24 on *www.heinemann .com*) that help them articulate their own perception of the author's central ideas. Sarah, writing about *Jacob,* realizes that Louise has to learn to "get along with what she has" before she can make the move to getting what she wants. She later writes, on her one-pager, that "This was a very deep and thought-provoking book. It made me think about our decisions in life and where they lead us." While Sarah did not think this novel was the best book she had ever read, she admits that, in the end, she learned from following Louise and thinking about her choices.

Kathy's one-pager asks students to put an image that somehow captures the essence of the book in the center of a page. Students may draw or capture images from the Internet (citing appropriately). Then, the student puts a specific element in each corner of the sheet: two passages that are personally meaningful because they are important to the story, one interpretive statement about what the student learned, and one comment about the student's personal response to the text. (See Figure 3–2 as an example.)

The Mandala activity introduces students to symbolism in a nonthreatening way. Kathy talks to students about the associations they have with different colors and then gives them a handout listing colors and the emotions or other abstractions they are often said to evoke. Then students are given a blank Mandala form (PTM 20 on *www .heinemann.com*) and the following instructions:

> Write the name of your character under the mandala. Then decide which of the characteristics you have identified are most important in this character. Keeping that in mind, begin to fill in your mandala with the colors that symbolize those characteristics. If the predominant characteristic of a character is confidence, for example, you may want to use more blue in the mandala or use blue mainly at the center of the graphic.
>
> Once you have completed your mandala, write one paragraph about your character in which you introduce the character, explain what each color

The Sign Of The Chrysanthemum

By Katherine Paterson

""It would be to dangerous to enter the forge trailing this," he said. Then he smiled.

In this way Muna of Awa became apprenticed to Fukuji of Nagano, master swordsmith of the capital. And the sword of Fukuji, which had been bounded to Muna's side, now hung on the sword wall unsheathed, so that any who entered the shop could read the motto engraved upon it:

"Through Fire Is The Spirit Forged.""

"To these will I abandon, will I entrust my life, The Great Creator, in the variety of his works, Blesses as well the lowly and the small, When all philosophy I resolve in this one act, I my stride the leviathan seas and they will not hold me:

Into the dark heart of all being I shall ride and dwell in the spacious hall of the ant."

From reading this book I learned that the things that you want, wouldn't always be perfect and the way you want them, and sometimes you have to live life the way you were born into it.

I enjoyed reading this book because it was full of excitement and adventure. With all the descriptive language, I felt that I was right there following Muna on his adventure.

FIGURE 3–2 *Joe's One-Pager on* The Sign of the Chrysanthemum

represents on the mandala, and the significance of its placement (for example, "Green is for renewal because Mrs. Mallard believed she was beginning a new life. This belief was the impetus for her change in attitude and thus is more dominant than the other colors"), and conclude the paragraph.

Reminder: Choose characteristics appropriate to the character, showing careful reading; a pattern of colors that is pleasing to the eye; effective paragraph organization, sentence fluency, and word choice; and attention to grammar and spelling convention.

Students love this activity and generate thoughtful, insightful designs with papers of explication that capture the complexities of Paterson's characters in surprising depth (see Figure 3–3).

FIGURE 3–3 *Joe's Mandala on* The Sign of the Chrysanthemum

Mandala

My main character is Muna. He is a very simplistic character, even if he went through several changes throughout the story. I used the four colors White, Black, Gray, and Brown. I chose the color white in my mandala to represent Muna in his youth. As a child he was always thinking about how he was going to change his name to a more respected name than "no name." By doing this shows how immature he was.

I used the colors black and gray to show how he matures through the story and becomes a man. In the story he sees himself as a man and chooses to keep the same name to show how much nobility he has. I used the color brown to show that he used to come from a poor town in Japan. He had no money at all when he started his trip and he was a peasant. But as he found a master he started to gain money.

Joe's mandala explanation

Jacob Have I Loved
by Katherine Paterson

Louise is a character with many different feelings. To describe her using four colors I chose the colors red, purple, green, and black. The black on the outer edges of the mandala represents the sadness and unhappiness wrapped around Louise's life. The black in the center of the mandala represents the mourning in her life. The green in the mandala represents the jealousy that Louise has for her perfect sister Caroline. I used the purple to symbolize the mystery that Louise is and the transformation that she goes through after she leaves Rass. The red in the mandala shows the aggression that Louise feels toward many people in her life. It also represents the war that is changing the world outside Rass and slowly changing things in Louise's life.

Sarah's mandala explanation

Mandala Type-Up

Muna is a very complex character whose emotions are always changing. However, I was able to find four colors that to me, best describe Muna's personality. The first color I chose was blue. I chose blue since it really demonstrates Muna's character traits of calmness and stability. Muna was able to stay calm after all the hardships he endured, and was able to stay stable enough to make it through them. The second color I chose was green. Green portrays the characteristics of health, youth, and generosity. These characteristics are shown in the story by how Muna is really healthy, how he is a child, and how generous he was to his friends, morally and financially. The next color I chose was yellow. I chose yellow since it showed Muna's hope, optimism, dishonesty, and betrayal. Muna always had the hope and optimism that he would find his father, and was always lying and betraying Fukuji, just for his benefit. The last color I chose was purple. Purple symbolizes mourning and transformation. The story shows these characteristics when Muna's mother dies, and him mourning her death, and when it shows Muna's transformation from a young, scared boy at the beginning of the story, to a grown up, confident man at the end of the story. In conclusion, as I stated earlier, Muna is a very complex character with many characteristics. I think I found the best colors to represent those characteristics, in the most eye-pleasing Mandala I could make using those four colors.

Dillon's mandala explanation

Note the differences in interpretation but the similarities of understanding about Muna in the two different mandalas about him. One student says Muna is complex; one says he is simple. But both discuss his growth over time and his process of maturing into manhood. Ruth, who read *Park's Quest* with Mary, shows through her Sketch-to-Stretch diary entry that she, too, understands the central action of the story and where its climax falls (see Figure 3–4).

Kathy's open-ended What If main character sentence starter activity also helps students think metaphorically (see PTM 25 on *www .heinemann.com*). Presented with statements such as "What kind of shoe is this person? Why?" or "If this person were a fruit, what kind would he or she be? Why?" students have to think not only about what kind of shoe the character would wear or what kind of fruit he or she might eat—often details provided in the novel—but they have to make connections and analogies. And then, provided with what is, in essence, a thesis statement, students have to support that generalization. Louise, then, according to Sarah, would be a lemon, "because she is so sour." Or she would be the metal object, a safe, "because they are so deep and hard to get into" (see Figure 3–5).

Diary Entry

Dear Diary,

I'm planning to go to find if my dad's name at the Vietnam Memorial in Washington D.C. I'm going to leave once my mom is heading for work. As you can see, I haven't told her that I was going to be leaving the house. So, hopefully, I get home before she does or else I might be in trouble. Well, got to go now! The earlier, the better.

Wish me luck!
Park

Sketch to Stretch Diary

~Park's Quest~

FIGURE 3–4 *Ruth's Sketch-to-Stretch and Diary Entry for* Park's Quest

Jacob Have I Loved
by Katherine Paterson

What If and Why

- If Louise was a time of day she would be night. I say this because she is so dark and even kind of goth.

- If Louise was a fruit she would be a lemon, because everyone hates her and she is so sour.

- If Louise was a shoe she would be a sneaker because she is a tomboy and is ready for anything.

- A metal item that represents Louise would be a safe. They are both very deep and hard to get into.

- If Louise was a car she would be a bus. She would be a bus because even though buses are kind of ugly they still have a purpose.

- If Louise could live in another time period she would live in the time period when the sun exploded. She would live here because she always is wishing she could die.

- A sound effect that would represent Louise would be one that is very quiet and uninteresting just like her.

- If Louise was a landform she would be a cavern because she is so dark and unpredictable.

- If Louise was a season she would be winter. She would be winter because she was so cold and harsh.

- One word to describe Louise would be strange. She is strange because sometimes she likes people and other times she hates them, like her sister for example.

FIGURE 3–5 *Sarah's What If Responses to* Jacob Have I Loved

Similarly, the structure of poetry forms, such as the cinquain or that of a story pyramid, allows students to creatively document their understanding of the heart of their reading. Joseph chooses to focus on Muna:

Muna

Poor, Determined

Searching, Sailing, Stealing

Muna Wants His Father

Samurai.

Dillon, however, is more interested in the motivations and character of Fukuji, so his cinquain captures what he believes is the essence of the swordmaker:

Fukuji

patient, charitable

forging, searching, assisting

helping Muna find father

guardian

Sarah, writing about *Jacob*, manages to evoke the essence of both Louise and her situation when she begins her story pyramid—Louise both lives on a small island, and the way Sarah phrases it, *is* a small island, alone in a sea of people who misjudge her. Sarah's last line shows how getting connected to the mainland allows Louise to connect to life in general:

Louise

Unpredictable, misjudged

A small island, Louise hates her life . . .

Louise moves to the mainland and gets a life.

Evaluating the Project

After the first literature circle cycle was completed, Kathy and Mary gave students a chance to self-evaluate and to evaluate the literature circle process. They provided students with a sheet titled *So How Did It Go?*

(PTM 26). After Kathy's students finished their extension activities and Mary's students finished the second round of literature circles, students evaluated the entire literature circle experience and also self-assessed their work. Kathy's students did this evaluation orally; Mary's students commented on sticky notes. Based on the student feedback, and their own observations of groups at work, as well as their assessment of student work, Kathy and Mary were able to evaluate what they did and what they would need to do in order to make future use of literature circles even more effective than this project.

In their reflections journal, Mary and Kathy write,

> Presenting Katherine Paterson and her rich, luscious novels to our students has been a very enjoyable and rewarding experience. What we need to do the next time we introduce Mrs. Paterson to our students is to thoroughly investigate Paterson's life. Both of us were stunned to find that she was a foster mom and saddened by the death of her son's friend. We were awed by her travels with missionary parents, but even more blown away by her ability to capture the places, so close to us, where she lived.

Both teachers felt that they initially did not know enough about Paterson to be able to guide students in making connections between her life and works. Being excellent role models, however, they continued researching while their students were engaged in the literature circle project, and when they found new material or came across new facts, shared these with the students who, as Mary said, "ate them up."

For instance, everyone appreciated knowing that Paterson wrote *The Great Gilly Hopkins,* which received the Newbery Honor, after she volunteered, in 1975, to be a foster parent for a pair of boys left homeless by the war in Cambodia. After several weeks, she was frustrated by their angry behavior and by her lack of ability to communicate with them, so that, when they left the Paterson home, she was relieved—but she also felt guilty that perhaps she had not given them everything she had to give. In *The Spying Heart,* Paterson says, "I found myself thinking, thank heaven this is only temporary. And what I was doing was regarding another human being as a disposable commodity. It took quite a while to realize that the funny book I wanted to write was buried in this tragic idea" (1989, 25).

While Kathy and Mary said they appreciated the fact that they were, in this process, modeling for students the habit in inquiry and the rewards of asking questions about a text and an author, they would, in the future, have the students work collaboratively to do author biography work that they would share with others as they present on their own particular novels.

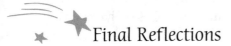

Final Reflections

As we sat talking about the experience of the Paterson literature circles, we agreed that while *Bridge to Terabithia* is often considered a book for elementary students, it is conceptually far more difficult than some of the other titles used. Lower-level students had difficulty with the metaphoric and symbolic aspects of the concept of *Bridge*, and Kathy will, in the future, allow her honors students to choose this title.

We also agreed that the literature circle process is highly effective; students, given the structure they need to read and respond to a text as well as the freedom to make sense of its multiple layers through collaboration with their peers, stay on task and are usually right on in their analysis. While Mary had to read out loud and use books on tape to help her lowest-level readers through *Field of Dogs*, the results were worth the effort. They felt good about themselves as students and readers, and they connected across racial boundaries in ways not typical in this class until this point in the year when they made pacts about how much of the book to read at a time, asked questions about the book they wanted to answer together, and worked on their projects.

At the same time, the fact that Mary and Kathy had to spend a great deal of time prepping students—not only about the concept of the literature circle and how to talk about books but also how to think outside the box in general—was discouraging. The students involved in this project were the first to come through the county school system under a curriculum that did not include literature circles and other reader-response strategies as a routine element. Thus, the teachers found that, in general, students were quite adept at responding to brief constructed response (BCR) questions, but questions that required imagination and synthesis were difficult for them. Several honors students initially reported *crying* because they were so uncomfortable with questions with no apparent right answer such as, "What kind of car would your character be and why?" As Kathy noted, "They can do analytical work. They've been taught a process for revisiting a text and finding information, but they can't get beyond that level of thinking without a lot of support and scaffolding that I didn't used to need to do."

These two master teachers are working in a data-driven decision-making environment. Students are assessed quarter by quarter; they have to complete brief constructed responses and so, to practice, the system now gives teachers sample BCRs based on the literature anthology that they have to use with their students, which means they need to use the anthology more faithfully than they would like. Students are tracked using tests that assess reading fluency using nonsense syllables and comprehension in timed chunks. The teachers have to prove that what they are doing in their classrooms is aligned with the assessments; they have to know the number of students who got an item correct and the number who got it wrong and they have to be able to outline the strategy they will use to help those who got something wrong to get it right the next time. To attend meetings about the "data," teachers are pulled out of class and so miss the opportunity to focus more attention on their struggling readers.

Mary bemoaned the situation saying, "I'm never allowed to do *anything* twice." In her eighth year of teaching, she's facing another new textbook this coming year. Kathy adds, "I feel like I'm cheating kids"—cheating them out of rich discussions, cheating them out of enrichment activities. She goes on, "*I* don't even like to touch the anthology because it's so heavy. How can kids possibly develop a love of literature if reading is such a physically oppressive task?" Mary jumps in with, "Give an anthology to a kid and he says 'ugh.' Give a novel to a kid and she says, 'OOOH.'"

Kathy provides an example. In the new textbook series The Language of Literature, by McDougal Littell, which she admits is better than the current one she has to use, there are questions such as, "Why do you think the editor chose this selection for the anthology?" She notes this is a hard question to answer if the reader has no knowledge of the entire work from which the selection in the anthology was taken. Would it not be better, Kathy ponders, to have a student read a whole novel or story or poem and then ask, "Which part would *you* choose as an excerpt, and why?" Or, "How would you label this selection in terms of theme?" might be better instead of asking, as the anthology does, "How does this selection fit within this thematic unit?"

Responses to Specific Titles

These teachers define their current teaching environment as one in which they must focus on teaching skills, whereas their own philosophy is about touching hearts. They want the freedom to be able to foster students' skill development while opening their hearts and minds so that they *want* to grow as readers and writers. They want the freedom to bring balance to their teaching, noting that the Maryland State Assessments (MSA) seems to counter their efforts to help students see the integration and connections among reading, writing, speaking, and listening—the first day of the MSA includes vocabulary and skill drill; "reading" is assessed on the second day. During the 2006–2007 academic year, the daily schedule at the middle level was revised so that English language arts teachers have an anthology block and a skill block focused on MSA score improvement. The idea of separating reading and literature from the skills is anathema to Kathy and Mary, who valued the Paterson project because they could foster reading as a leisure time activity choice while also developing writing, thinking, and discussion skills.

As a result of their experiences, both teachers want to find ways to use their assigned anthologies for literature circle purposes. They find it odd that while they are encouraged to use group work and to teach students how to cooperate, they do not feel that students are being guided as well as in the past about how to function as a group. They had to consciously help the students make decisions that they thought would be routine. Mary says, "We have to learn how to take the curriculum we're given and teach the students what's really important." The students' responses to the novels they chose to read document that they are able to meet curricular outcomes using the literature circles approach.

Park's Quest

One of Mary's classes was an inclusion class that she team-taught with a special education teacher. Several young men with widely divergent reading abilities ended up grouped together on this book. Mary reports,

"My special education colleague and I *fought* to go listen to their discussions. Two kids took their parents to the Vietnam Memorial after reading the book. One kid went to his father and begged him to talk about his experiences in the war, which he did. Their own questions about this book are *deep*; they're ticked at the ending and they want a sequel." It was exciting to hear the two students who visited the Vietnam Memorial talk about touching the wall of stone and tracing the names of the dead as Park did, to hear them describe how they "felt the connection" to the soldiers and the past and to Park. Kathy notes that she was able to draw in a recent immigrant from Vietnam by asking for help with pronunciation, and so learned that it's not "Fan" but "T'un."

The Sign of the Chrysanthemum

Mary and Kathy chose this book because it is short; because it is about the samurai culture, which is appealing to middle school boys; and because it is about identity development in such explicit ways. Again, a student who was a recent immigrant from Japan was able to feel like part of the class in new ways when he brought in his grandfather's sword and picture. His grandfather was a samurai and the student contributed to his peers' understanding of the book from his cultural heritage. One student reported, "The author's message is that you should never give up. Even if you don't find exactly what you're looking for, try hard enough, and you may find something better, just like Muna." Students also felt comforted by the ending when Muna was able to "find a family" because he learned to "face the truth."

Jacob Have I Loved

This title was the least well received. Several girls helped Mary unpack the books and they were attracted, initially, to the cover and the idea of a book about sisters. But they had difficulty with Louise and could not connect with her as a character because of her neediness. They found her relationship with the Captain "yucky." Kathy had thought her honors class would relate to *Jacob* because of its setting. They live on Maryland's western shore; the peninsula is still populated with watermen whom they can see crabbing, fishing, and oystering; they are a ferry ride away from the islands Paterson used as the model for Rass Island, the novel's setting. But, the contemporary student population of the county now reflects, primarily, the explosive growth of the Patuxent River Naval Air Station, and students often have little interaction with the water-based parts of the economy and the older lifestyle of the watermen. So, the teachers found they had to do much more building of prior knowledge about the environment than anticipated, and the historical nature of the book also meant they needed to do more scaffolding than expected. Kathy noted that she was reminded, "Readability level does not reflect reading maturity level." The teachers now wish they had chosen to use *The Same Stuff as Stars* instead of *Jacob*.

On the other hand, one of Mary's students, a young man labeled emotionally disturbed and possibly autistic, but who is off-the-charts smart, chose *Jacob*. Mary was concerned but he participated in a group with four young women. He did, in fact, like the book and did, in fact, connect to the setting, zeroing in on what he saw as the book's focus: "the oystermen and how they work and how that affects the rest of their lives." The reminder to all of us as teachers here is that it is difficult to predict how or why a young person might respond to a book. As Mary says, "The more books we can make available to them and the more choices we can give them, the more likely it is that they'll find something to read that will pull them in and compel them forward—and then we can teach them any skill we like."

The Great Gilly Hopkins

This book was a big hit. But, Mary and Kathy both found it disturbing how many of their students could relate to Gilly on the point of promises unkept by adults in their lives. Mary said, "I was moved to choking" by the response of one of her students, a self-described bad-ass who'd once threatened Mary. This same young woman passionately argued, "It's not about hope—it's about *love*, Mrs. C. It's about love for Trotter. It's about Gilly's love for herself." In recounting this conversation, Mary was teary-eyed, saying, "She *got* it, dammit. She *got* it. This is what teaching can and should be all about."

Preacher's Boy

The male readers *loved* this book. They related to the plot from the opening scene of petticoats flying on the flag pole, and they had spirited discussions about doing the right thing. Pa, in *Preacher's Boy,* tells Robbie, "I hope it will be a good century. . . . I want my children and grandchildren to grow up in a world where people have learned to think with their minds and hearts and not with weapons of destruction" (2001, 167–68). Students want the same things for themselves and yet recognize the chaos in the world around them and wonder what Pa and Robbie would make of our current international involvements. Mary states, "My curriculum requires coverage of concepts such as *biography,* and *theme,* requires attention to skills such as character analysis and requires a focus on genres, such as poetry. In the discussions of *Preacher's Boy,* my students dealt with all of these topics in painless ways. They analyzed character and talked about theme and responded to the poetry of the language and I didn't have to force a thing."

Conclusion

Paterson writes,

> We are fearful, we adults, and we want to know what they read and why they read and if they don't understand what that Ferris wheel symbolizes in the first sentence of *Tuck Everlasting* we give them a C minus. It doesn't count that the child loved the book and was able because of it to face his own mortality a little more bravely. We're so occupied with our own agenda for their reading that we forget more important things. We forget the power a book may have for a child which is quite apart from the literal or even figurative understanding of the text. We want children to get from the book what *we got* from the book, forgetting the wisdom of readers of whatever age to choose from a book that which is appropriate for their own lives. (1990, 15)

Fisher (2001) notes that Paterson fits the model of writers who use their writing to add something to the world; Paterson does not want to maintain the status quo. Her work "serves as a powerful example of how writing can stimulate conversation about previously taboo topics and, by providing a forum for such discussions, can become part of a force that changes society" (177).

Paterson, addressing the Swedish Parliament, stated

I have always been taught that the evils of the world are the result of sin, but perhaps we should consider that poverty, disease, crime and war also result from a failure of the human imagination. We cannot fully imagine ourselves as victims of injustice, nor can we fully imagine how wrongs of injustice might be righted. A novel can illumine the imagination because it lets us experience another person's life at a very deep level—it allows us to eavesdrop on another person's soul.

When Abraham Lincoln was introduced to Harriet Beecher Stowe, the author of *Uncle Tom's Cabin*, he is quoted as saying: "So this is the little woman who wrote the book that made this big war." My dream is that someday a novelist will be greeted with the words: "So this is the person who wrote the book that helped heal the world."

I think this is what many writers are seeking to do. The results are not as dramatic as the reactions to *Uncle Tom's Cabin* a hundred and fifty years ago, but healing happens in many small ways. The essayist Barry Lopez speaks eloquently about the power of the story to heal—"to repair a spirit in disarray." The task of fiction he says, is to "illumine and make whole." To heal means to make whole. This is more than patching up, putting a bandage on a wound. It is more than simple catharsis, the purging of the emotions. Healing here is concerned with growing, with becoming. And that is why children's books are so important. We don't come into this world fully human. We become human, we become whole, and the stories we hear and read as children are vital nourishment in this process of becoming fully human. (Paterson 2006c)

Mary and Kathy are the kind of teachers whom Paterson would be happy to have partner with her in bringing books to students. Their literature circles project created the space and time for students to connect with Paterson's books in ways that helped them enrich their imaginations, better understand themselves and others, and, in that way, feel the sense of healing and becoming Paterson wants to provide.

Guys Night Out and
Come Sing, Jimmy Jo

The Context

Lou D'Ambrosio is a special education teacher by training who has developed a passion for connecting young men with books because of his own personal story. As a child growing up without a father, Lou found solace in the pages of good stories, and he continues to enjoy talking about what he has read with his mother and brothers. At Milton Somers Middle School, where he was teaching during 2004–2005, he partnered with a language arts teacher, Todd Narehood, to create the Guys Night Out program, funded in part by a grant from *The Washington Post*. The school is a big one, housing approximately four hundred students over its limit through the use of twenty trailers. It is home to a mixed population in terms of ethnic diversity, and serves many students who qualify for free or reduced-priced lunches. At the time of the program's inception, reading scores for the students in general had not been rising as much as teachers and administrators would have liked.

The school had tried using a summer reading academy to promote reading skill development. But that program, designed to motivate middle school students as readers, was quite regimented and scripted. Students invited into the program were those just below cut-off scores in reading tests as defined for adequate yearly progress; the hope was that with more support, they would then be able to test above the cut-off point in the following year. However, in talking with students, Lou realized that reading is not viewed as a particularly guy sort of activity, which contributed to the lack of motivation and investment on the part of the male participants in the summer program, as did its regimented nature. Thus, reading scores for male students who participated in the program did not tend to reflect growth in the same way scores of the female participants did. Lou also realized that many young men, too, have fathers who want to be supportive but who, because of long work hours or lack of role models themselves, are not sure how best to support their sons in their academic and literacy endeavors.

The Inception of Guys Night Out

Thus began Guys Night Out. The goals of this program were to bring fathers—or other adult male role models of significance in the lives of young men in sixth grade—together with their sons through a guys' book club, and to promote enhanced reading fluency and comprehension in the process. Students were nominated for invitation into the group by their teachers, who were asked to give Lou a list of any sixth-grade developmental boy who "does not like to read, is difficult to motivate, and could benefit from a literacy connection with other influential males."

Lou is a big guy—an athlete, a weight lifter, a former college football player—who has the ability to impress his students through his awards for athletic prowess; yet, he loves books and is willing to spend time talking about them. He recognizes that his presence and his qualities help young men view reading as OK. In its second year, the 2005–2006 academic year, the program brought together eight pairs of fathers or adult men and the young male students of importance to them. All of the students tested two to three grade levels below their sixth-grade status on standardized tests of grade-level reading ability. A condition of participation in the program was that the student had to bring a significant adult male to each meeting. In most cases, the boys brought their fathers, but two of the adults were not fathers but the boyfriends of the mothers of the students; one of these individuals traveled faithfully from Washington DC, driving more than one hour each time, to be part of the Guys Night Out with a young man who participates in the emotional adjustment program.

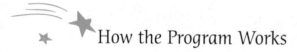

How the Program Works

The group meets for three months, one night per month. Midway through each month, Lou meets with the students during the sixth-grade lunch period to find out how far they have progressed with reading the book of the month. *Come Sing, Jimmy Jo* by Katherine Paterson was the third and final book the group shared as readers, and they held their last Guys Night Out session on May 4, 2006.

Each meeting of the group lasts ninety minutes. Each meeting follows the same pattern of activities. First, the guys cook and eat; that happens between 6 and 6:45 P.M. One time, the female principal of the school came to the meeting and cooked spaghetti for the group, but then she was banished for the book conversation time, which starts at 6:45. Then Lou and Todd spark discussion by asking open-ended questions to provoke response, after which they try to stop talking, unless the conversation comes to a lull.

Sometimes, the group leaders ask a question designed to provoke readers into making connections between themselves and the world of the story. For instance, their first book of the year was *Skinny Bones* (Park 2006). Lou raised the question, "Imagine you're a superhero. What five traits would you want to have?" After allowing both sons and fathers to reply, he asked, "So how does this question relate to the book?" Alex, a/k/a "Skinny-Bones" may be the smallest player on his baseball team, but he has the biggest mouth. That trait gets him into trouble when he talks himself into a pitching contest.

Typically, though, the group leader starts the discussion by asking a father to summarize a part of the book that he and the son particularly enjoyed, after which the father asks the student to elaborate and add details. The conversation flows from there, without an agenda, and without explicit attention to any specific curricular goals or without any attempt on the part of the group leaders to achieve specific insights about the book. The idea is to get the older and younger men talking, as readers, about the characters, plots, and themes of the novels in ways that then allow them to talk about issues of importance to their lives outside of the group.

Usually the evening ends with a game. They might play a book-based game, such as Inside/Outside the Bag. The reader becomes a character and tells the other group members what they can see of the character, using descriptors from the book. Then the reader has to make inferences, telling the rest of the group what they cannot see, what the character keeps hidden, inside the bag. Sometimes the game is just for fun. Fruit Salad involves having one person in the middle of a ring of chairs, standing, while everyone else is seated. Everyone thinks of a fruit, and the person in the middle calls out the names of fruits—when the fruit is called out that corresponds to the fruit one of the seated participants is thinking about, that person has to stand up and scramble to find another place to sit, while the person in the middle also tries to sit. The kids and fathers both like this game and delight in researching odd, unusual fruits so that they can stump each other.

Sometimes the game is designed to promote thought about what it means to be a man, as well as to encourage connection. For instance, the group played a game derived from Inuit traditions that involves having the men and boys line up facing each other. First a father walks down the line of young men portraying his "hunter" face, staring into the eyes of each young man in turn for at least thirty seconds. If the father breaks, he is "captured" by the sons. If the son "breaks," he is captured by the other side. Then the first in line for the boys walks down the line of fathers, also staring into the eyes of each man in turn, trying to remain centered, focused, calm, and confident. The idea of the game section of the evening is to do something fun, together, that creates a bond among the group members and that, upon occasion, provides insight into the world of a story the group has read.

Additionally, the Guys Night Out crew earns T-shirts. On the back, each shirt has an open book with hands on the sides. Names of the fathers and sons who participated are listed on one page of the book. On the other page of the book it reads, "Real Men Read"; underneath this heading is a list of the books they shared. The students were able to choose the colors for these shirts, and they decided on ash gray shirts with navy lettering because these are their school colors; therefore, they were able to wear them on school spirit days. The school's principal paid for the shirts and donated toward the food for the meals.

Lou and Todd selected *Come Sing, Jimmy Jo* from among the whole range of Paterson titles for Guys Night Out. When I first learned that this was their choice, I was intrigued because the book is not the first one that came to my mind when we were talking about using a Paterson novel with Lou's struggling middle school readers. I had imagined that *Field of the Dogs*, with its themes of bullying and loyalty and its more plot-driven nature might be selected. But Lou described his reasons for choosing to share Jimmy Jo's story in persuasive fashion. The plot of the novel hinges on the fact that James has been told that he's got the gift, and he does love to sing except that every time he thinks about standing in front of people, singing with his guitar, he feels ill. But now his family is depending on him, and he's got to find the courage to face the audience and his parents. Lou knew that while some of the students who would participate in the program were athletes and while some were out-of-doors enthusiasts, he also knew he had at least one student for whom participation in musical events was at the heart of his identity. And he knew he had some other students whose talents and interests were sometimes perceived as nerdy. He also wanted to see if the group participants could engage in discussion that spoke to interconnections among titles, and thought the fact that *Come Sing, Jimmy Jo* had a different kind of plot would make for richer intertextual conversation.

 ## The *Come Sing, Jimmy Jo* Night

After dinner on the evening of the *Come Sing, Jimmy Jo* reading, Todd tossed out his preliminary question, "I just want some preliminary feedback about our book tonight. I know it was longer than our other books, but I know you made it through. So, what did you think?"

Derek responded quickly, saying, "I liked it because of the music; it's a good book because I do music and I'm really into it so I could . . . I related to Jimmy Jo." Stephen reacted to Derek by noting that, "I'm not a good reader and I'd kind of lose my place, and the book seemed long and I didn't think I could finish. I did kinda like it, but I wish it had been shorter. Why did you relate to Jimmy Jo so much?"

Derek then elaborated. He talked about how much time he spends practicing his instrument each day, and said, "And I put myself into the music the way Jimmy Jo does," to which Stephen responded, "That's cool. That's cool."

But then Jackson brought up a different perspective, saying, "I couldn't really understand it and I didn't really like it, the way they were talking made it hard for me to understand them." At this point, some of the fathers joined in the conversation, reacting to Jackson's comments on the language of the story. Paterson uses Appalachian dialect to set the family apart from some of the other characters in the book, and some of the adults in the group also found this use of dialect problematic. James' father agreed but offered another view, stating, "I like music as much as anyone. But as an adult to read it, I thought the language would keep kids from getting as much out of it as they could. Once you got used to the way they were talking and what was happening, I fell in love with certain characters and hated other ones, and then I definitely wanted to keep coming back to it." James added, "Yeah, once I got into it, I liked the story."

Building on the comments about language, Travis' father added, "I sorta liked the language, and I liked the way the characters interacted and the way Jimmy Jo interacted with his grandmother." The introduction of the character of the grandmother sparked the group leader to talk about his own connections to that aspect of the story. He added, "I really enjoyed the opening of the book, with the grandmother loading tobacco into her pipe, and I sort of connected it with *Huck Finn*, another book with a lot of dialect about a kid finding himself. And I liked the themes— how Jimmy Jo had to make hard choices, the connection with his grandmother, and the family." Jackson then noted that the grandmother was his favorite character, how she was a gutsy lady, and how she reminded him of older women, aunts, in his own family. Travis' dad noted, "We first started reading it when we went camping, and we were reading it out loud, and when you read it out loud the dialect makes more sense and you can keep track better of who was talking, and my own grandmother talks like that, so I could hear her in my head as I was reading." Stephen chimed in with, "That's a good idea, reading it out loud. I gotta try that."

Lou pushed the conversation to a consideration of theme at this point. "The grandmother was like his protector, but then he had to leave, and so Jimmy Jo had to stand on his own and figure out who he was in his family with his mom and dad. The whole relationship with his dad and how his dad wouldn't admit the song was his—what would you do?" While not everyone initially felt that they could relate to Jimmy Jo, *all* the group participants—both older and younger group members— had something to say about this topic. Reading *Come Sing, Jimmy Jo* with their fathers or significant adult male role models encouraged the students, whose reading skills were ordinarily less sophisticated than many of their peers, to engage in lively responses.

One dad commented, "My own mom was totally supportive and always screaming for me at games, but this mom threw him to the wolves. This was a much more serious book, and made me think how not all kids have supportive parents." He asked how the athletes felt about their parents and the ways they get support, and the students jumped in, noting that, "They're OK!" and Derek elaborated, saying, "I wouldn't be anywhere near where I am if I didn't have my parents. I play soccer, and my uncle is the coach, and my mom tells me I can do better in school so she helps me and now I'm doing better." Thomas added, "It's your folks paying for gas and taking you to games out of their own time, so even if they're not cheering, they're helping you."

A father threw out a question that took these personal comments back to the story, asking, "If your parents not only didn't give you the money and didn't drive you, but also told you were no good, how would you be different?" The students started talking to each other, and eventually Derek said, "It'd just be really hard. I don't know how Jimmy Jo could keep on going out there to perform every day." And then Thomas added, "Yeah, he was strong."

Lou then tried to get the conversation focused on particular segments of the story by asking, "What was your favorite part of this book?"

Derek, the musician in the crowd, immediately said, "I would try to hear him when he was singing, try to imagine his voice—all sweet; I liked when he was singing." This young man was reading imaginatively, trying to imagine the voice of the character. Thomas responded, indicating he, too, was reading imaginatively, by saying he tried to imagine getting out on stage in front of all those people, and liked how Jimmy Jo could just "do it. His family's really depending on him, so that really ups the pressure. They need the money he can bring in. What if he didn't do well and then they couldn't eat? I don't think I could do that."

The conversation diverted for a while as the group shared stories of stage fright; there was much camaraderie and laughing. But then Travis' father brought the group back to the novel, and asked, "Dads, would you want your boys to be the provider, bringing in the paychecks? I wouldn't be comfortable with that. It's not just the pride and not being the bread-winner—it's the idea of putting him out there and not protecting him." Stephen's dad said, "It's hard because you want to be proud of the talent and want him to go out and really do something with it, and you want him to have confidence and make something of his gift, but how far do you go?" Thomas' father offered, "How about Tiger Woods? His dad was a golfer, and he's just passed away, but he—no, he was a minor league baseball player—and then he *knew* when Tiger was just a little kid, he realized that as a dad, he had to support him with his whole heart." And Thomas added, "If I had a son, I'd just want him to be happy."

There was general consensus that it was understandable how Jimmy's father and mother felt jealousy. Derek's father chimed in with, "A lot of it comes from how you're raised. It'd be difficult if you're in a field all your life, and then your child comes along and outperforms you, that's hard. I can understand how you'd be jealous, but you *have* to be the parent and be supportive and do what's good for the child." Jackson said, "Yeah, I'd be really jealous, too." It is important to note that Jackson, up to this point in the evening, had not been as active a participant as some of the other group members; he had commented early on that the language made reading the book difficult, but he was able, with the help of this group conversation, to take the perspective of the parent in the novel, and he later noted that the discussion made him like the book more than he initially thought he liked it. James summed up this part of the conversation by saying, "His mom hated the fact that he was so good—that's a hard pill to swallow—but if it's family, you have to be supportive."

This comment, about what *family* means, led one of the dads to make an intertextual connection. Travis' dad said, "All these books are about family. There are three different structures [kinds of family relationships] in the three books—in one, the parents ultimately helped the son; next book, tough love. Here, the mom is totally jealous of her little boy." Derek's father agreed, "It is nice to see different family situations and different family relationships. I didn't really see how all three books connected until we started talking about them, so it's neat to see that they relate to each other." Stephen contributed, "Yeah, it gave me a different perspective. It made me think about my parents differently and appreciate them more and think more about what I want to do for my son some day. I didn't get that just from the first two books."

Lou began to wind down this part of the evening and asked for an overall evaluation of the book in a very concrete way that the students could understand. He wanted to know whether these readers would keep *Come Sing, Jimmy Jo* if the Guys Night Out program was funded for the following year. Travis asked, "Do we always stick with sixth graders? I would keep it but I'd do it with eighth graders." Pushed to say why, Travis said it was a "harder" book than some of the others, which he defined as both longer and as having more difficult language, and he thought maybe eighth graders would be more able to handle it. He also said that the "stuff" of the book, the relationships Jimmy Jo has to negotiate and the choices he has to make, might be something "older kids would relate to more." James jumped in and said that he would keep the book, pointing out to Travis that they all managed to read the whole thing, and added, "It's good to learn about different parts of the country and different kinds of families, and how families are different and the same, you know, in all the emotions that get riled up." Jackson said, "But even though the story is OK and we could read it, I'd give it to eighth graders because the reading is harder."

Jackson's mentor asked if the group could do an animal book instead. Travis asked an interesting question, "Why do we just read about boys?" Lou asked, in return, "What's this program called?" Travis answered, "Well, it's Guys Night Out but we don't have to read just about guys. Animals are good. Or, you could do one of those Lion, Witch and Wardrobe books. They've got good adventure plots. You don't have to read the whole book—you could skip around." Thomas then noted, "But our books were all about family. We could do that book where the kid has an older brother who got in trouble. That's shorter but it's still about a family and relationships. The Narnia books aren't so much about family." (Lou believed Thomas was referring to *Miracle's Boys* by Jacquelyn Woodson, but Thomas was not sure of the title.)

Travis' dad commented that maybe it would be good to still read about Jimmy Jo, but maybe sandwich the Paterson title between the other two books, and thus end the year with one of the funnier, less serious books. Derek's father added that he, too, would keep the book, noting, "It's got a lot to talk about in it and maybe we could've used some more introduction to it." Lou asked him what he meant. Derek said, "Like my one English teacher, who was really good, would ask us questions or play some music or do an activity before we started a book in class so that the book wasn't so just 'out there' when we finally started reading." Derek's father said that is what he meant: "Maybe if we knew it'd be Appalachian dialect and practiced with it first, or listened to some country music, that would've helped."

Stephen went back to the question about whether to keep the book, noting, "Now that I think about it, it's better to keep this book last because we built up to it. We had things to compare it to while we were reading and we were used to reading together, so we could talk about things more easily." The fathers of James and Thomas concurred. They added that they liked having a serious book to read. James' father says, *"Skinny Bones* was fun, and it's good to know reading can be fun," and then Thomas' father continues, "But it's also good to read and think about something new because of the characters you get to know." And remember Jackson, who found the book difficult to read and to get into? He says, "Yeah, that's true."

Connections with Literary Theory

It is interesting that the participants of the Guys Night Out program, without much guidance, and without much teacher prodding, interacted with *Come Sing, Jimmy Jo* in ways that reflect an array of literary theories. As their discussion flowed, they focused on traditional structural elements, using the language of formalism in making comments about characterization, theme, plot, setting, and Paterson's use of language. They thought about whether characters seemed realistic, and talked about the value of the author's use of dialect, even while acknowledging the difficulties this caused them as readers.

However, much of the discussion reflected reader-response theory, which defines reading as a transaction between reader and text. As John Noell Moore writes, "Reader-response approaches consider the ways in which we respond personally to texts and how our personal history gets embedded in the text. . . . All reader-response theories see the reader as an active participant in the creation of the text, so our interpretation arises out of the ways in which we weave ourselves into the text as we read it" (1997, 12–13).

Comments about how certain characters, such as Jimmy Jo's grand-mother, reminded readers of their own grandparents, or comments that indicated that readers were trying to enter into Jimmy Jo's world of expe-rience—imagining his voice, or imagining his fear as he faced an audi-ence—reflected a reader-response–based approach to the text. The lengthy discussion about what children might expect from their parents in terms of support is a good example of how this particular text opened up in a way it otherwise might not have opened because in this setting, fathers and sons were reading together. And, the way the discussion took note of contemporary culture, with references to Tiger Woods, and, albeit briefly, considered how Paterson's novel relates to other novels shows that, without being taught to do so, these readers have an intu-itive handle on the value of taking a cultural studies approach. In their desire for some scaffolding on which to hang their reading of the text—asking for a chance to listen to some country music or study Appalachian language traits—at least some of these readers recognize the need to put the text into conversation with the larger cultural context it reflects (Moore 1997, 164).

Changes in Readers

In addition to documenting qualitatively how participating in the Guys Night Out program affected the young men in the group, all the students in the group completed an Adolescent Motivation to Read pre-post program study. It included twenty questions addressing their perceptions of how their friends view them as readers, how they view themselves as readers, how they feel about reading in general, how they perceive individuals who identify themselves as readers, and how they behave as readers. On the last night of the program, two sets of fathers and sons were not present; one father was out of town doing training for his job, while another father works undercover and did not want his voice on tape.

The six students who completed the post-participation survey self-reported no downward turns in their perceptions, with the exception of one item, and reported increased confidence, appreciation of reading as a valuable activity, and increased willingness to respond to books and to talk about their reading with others. Half of them felt that their friends viewed them in May as "good readers," whereas in February, they felt they were perceived as "OK" or "poor" readers. As opposed to February, when two-thirds of them reported that they "never" or "almost never" told friends about any good books they were reading, in May, they reported that they tell their friends about good books either "some of the time" or "a lot." They reported that they moved from either "never" thinking of an answer when a teacher asked them about what they had read, or "having trouble" thinking of answers, to being able to think of answers "sometimes" or "always." They also reported that when in a group talking about reading, they now "almost always share their ideas" instead of, as in the past, reporting that they "almost never talk about" their ideas. Two-thirds of these young men moved from thinking of reading as "a boring way to spend time" to viewing it as "a great way to spend time," and they envisioned spending at least "some of my time" reading as an adult. And, they felt, by May, that they would be at least "sort of happy" to receive a book as a present.

On one item, responses went down. Item 7 on the survey was, "When I am reading by myself, I understand (a) almost everything I read; (b) some of what I read; (c) almost none of what I read; or (d) none of what I read." Interestingly, all of the students initially checked that they understand "almost everything I read." On the post-program survey, none of them checked this item; instead, they checked response b: some of what I read. On the surface, this change could be viewed as indicative of a failing on the part of the program. However, this change actually can be viewed as not so disheartening. The students—and their fathers—voiced the perception that talking about the books made them realize that there were points they missed when reading on their own. Derek's father stated, "It took a little while to get into the book because of the language barrier, the Appalachian dialect, but I had a bit of trouble trying to find out where it was going, but then it started picking up and I really enjoyed it for a while, but then I couldn't figure out where it was heading. I thought it was about average. But now I think it's a lot better than I thought; it's got more to it and I think I missed some important things about Jimmy's character and I like it better now that I have a fuller picture of it." Jackson said, "Me too." One of the values of participation on the Guys Night Out program seems to be that the student participants also begin to realize that they are not reading with impeccable comprehension, and so, on item 7, they perhaps are showing a new, more realistic, awareness of their reading skills.

Eight pairs of readers is not a significant sample size, and it is not possible to generalize in any meaningful way from the results of six sets of pre-post surveys. But, it seems clear that the young men and their fathers or male role models involved in Guys Night Out clearly benefited from having a community of readers in which to talk about books in an informal, nonthreatening manner.

Lou, as the teacher and group leader, also found participation in this program enjoyable. He liked the fact that the group could take the book conversation in any direction that it wanted; he liked the fact that he was just one reader within the group, able to share his own responses and to learn from the other group members rather than having to worry about assessing student progress. What all the teachers involved in this project have, rather wistfully, noted is that they believe students learn more, become better readers, and invest more of themselves in their reading when they have choices about what to read, how to read, and why to do so. They are eloquent in articulating the value for students in being part of a community of readers—in which the teacher is also a member, offering insights and information that can help shape students' interactions with texts without imposing too much upon the students' thoughts and feelings in ways that eventually turn them off to reading.

Other teachers who use this novel might want to know that *Come Sing, Jimmy Jo* grew out of Paterson's own struggle, as a very shy person, to adjust to sudden fame. "I remembered my junior high days and a girl in my class called Anita Carter. Anita was painfully shy. But that wasn't why none of us knew how to treat her. The problem was that she was also famous—being a country music singer with her mother MayBelle and her two older sisters. In my own little struggle with 'celebrity,' I began to think about how hard it must have been for Anita who was so shy in school and such a star on stage." Paterson goes on to say that later in her life, she received a note from Anita, who had read the book and enjoyed it, but told the author that she couldn't picture the young Katherine. Paterson notes, "Of course she couldn't. In the story of her life, I was the totally forgettable Will Short" (Paterson 2006b).

Paterson writes that her experience is that there are kids who don't read well, and those who don't read a lot—but mostly she thinks children can be the most wonderful of readers "willing not only to suspend disbelief but eager to give their whole lives to enter imaginatively into the story. They like to be entertained, of course, we all do, but they also enjoy being stretched. A great number of them seem not only willing to dig below the surface, they seem delighted to" (1990, 4). In *The Spying Heart* Paterson says, "The growth of imagination demands windows. Windows through which we can look out at the world and windows through which we can look into ourselves" (1989, 61). Paterson would have liked the way her creation, Jimmy Jo, and his story opened up windows for the fathers and sons of Guys Night Out.

Teaching *Lyddie* and *Jacob Have I Loved* as American Historical Fiction

Summaries

Jacob Have I Loved: Growing up on isolated Rass Island during WWII, Louise is bitter that her younger twin, more beautiful and talented, though fragile, seems to get everything she wants and needs, while "Wheeze" has to fend for herself. This story of sibling rivalry ends in reconciliation once Louise comes to understand her family, herself, and her own hidden talents.

Lyddie: When Lyddie's family farm is so deeply in debt that she is hired out, Lyddie experiences both the hardships but also the economic independence that working in the mills of nineteenth-century Massachusetts afforded. But she then has to make choices about what is truly important to her.

Getting Started

As previously mentioned, when teaching Children's and Young Adult Literature and Other Materials for Teaching Reading, I try to model strategies that my students, future teachers of middle and secondary school English language arts, will be able to adapt for use as teachers. I want them to experience strategies they can use to make their classrooms places in which all students both can find their way into stories and can find some connection between the world of adolescence and the larger themes and concepts important to the organizational structure and mandated core learning goals that guide the Maryland English language arts curriculum. In the past I've used Karen Hesse's Newbery Award–winning *Out of the Dust* (1997) as a central novel for a unit on American Fiction as a way to illustrate for my future teachers how young adult literature can be woven into standard curricular organizational schemes. In recent years I have been using Paterson's *Lyddie* because I wanted to take my students further back in time while considering the nature of historical fiction and also introducing them, at least in a rudimentary way, to concepts of feminist literary theory. A former student, Betsy Gardiner, paralleled this unit using *Jacob Have I Loved*, which was on the St. Mary's County Public Schools approved reading list for tenth graders. A bonus chapter about her experiences is available on *www.heinemann.com* in a section titled "Using *Jacob Have I Loved* in the High School English Classroom."

For this unit, my students all read *Lyddie* and *Jacob Have I Loved*. Then they choose one other book to read from a list of complementary texts as we engage in discussions of weaving young adult literature into the typical eleventh-grade curriculum in Maryland, which involves most frequently a survey of American literature from Crèvecoeur through contemporary times. These complementary texts include *Out of the Dust* by Karen Hesse, *Staying Fat for Sarah Byrns* by Chris Crutcher, *Hush* by Jacqueline Woodson, *The Year of the Gopher* by Phyllis Reynolds Naylor, *A Solitary Blue* by Cynthia Voigt, *The Land* by Mildred Taylor, and *Heroes* by Robert Cormier.

My goal for this unit is to provide students with an opportunity to read three young adult novels, two of which they read in common with their peers, while they become experts on one additional title, responsible for sharing their insights through Slavin's "jigsaw" strategy (1995). What is heartening to me is that, having experienced the power of this cooperative learning technique for themselves, my future teachers report that they then are able to structure similar cooperative experiences for their own students. They also report that they appreciate the fact that, through the jigsaw groups, they gain secondhand knowledge of several other quality American young adult titles that they then can share with their students in meaningful ways.

Initiating the jigsaw strategy involves students working with others who selected the same title for their independent reading choice. In these expert groups, readers share their reactions to their chosen text, work with their colleagues to respond to any questions or activities I pose, determine important questions they have about the novel, and make decisions about the key elements of the story and the author's craft that they want to pass along to students who have not read their title.

After these groups have done their work, I regroup the students so that, in each newly formed group, there is at least one "expert" for each of the texts we are using. Depending on the size of the class, there may be two experts for a given title in a group—or a group may be missing an expert for a title. But, in general, in these second-phase groups, at least four titles are represented and, as the experts overview their novels, the group as a whole must complete activities or respond to questions designed to foster intertextual dialogue. In the American Fiction unit, the titles reflect a variety of time periods in American history, and there is a mix of male and female protagonists. Thus, for the most part, after reading reviews or hearing my booktalks about the titles, most students find at least one novel about which they can generate some enthusiasm for reading. Once, a student who was a Revolutionary War buff and who participated in historical reenactments, asked to read an Anne Rinaldi title about this time period instead of one on my list, and I said yes.

 ## Bridging into the Unit

We usually begin this unit by talking about *Lyddie,* which everyone has read prior to the first class session for the unit. I introduce the novel early in the semester when I model the concept of *bridges,* emphasizing the need for teachers to create a scaffold for their students that will activate their cognitive structures and help them become ready to read, both emotionally and intellectually. I start by showing the students a series of props from my home that somewhere include the word *industrial* in their product descriptions—cleaning products often are labeled "industrial grade" or "industrial strength." I ask them what this adjective means and then ask them to write a paragraph describing an industrial setting or any personal experiences they have had working or touring such settings.

Then I ask them to create a web on the word *revolution*; we generate synonyms for the word (*war, change, disruption, overthrow*) as well as words that seem to relate to the term (*revolve, evolution*), examples of revolutions they have studied or experienced, and reasons why such abrupt changes happen. At this point, we tie the terms *industrial* and *revolution* together. Students work with a partner to write a one-sentence definition of the Industrial Revolution in the United States. They share their responses, and I ask them to consider what it would have been like to be an adolescent at the time the country was experiencing industrialization. That question usually leads to the generation of other questions as the students realize they do not really know what industries sprang into being, where industrialization began, where it spread, or what conditions were like in these new, industrial settings. Students use the Internet or library resources I provide in the classroom to learn the dates for the Industrial Revolution in the United States, to find out in which states this revolution took place, and to answer any other questions they think would help them to answer in getting ready to read a novel set during this transformational time period. We also share any pictures of photographs we find that bring the Industrial Revolution to life.

We end this introductory phase of the unit by making predictions about what *Lyddie* will be about, knowing that it is set during the Industrial Revolution. Typically, students assume the novel will be about one young woman, whom they predict will be emotionally strong but who will undergo significant changes in her life. They assume Lyddie will have to move from a relatively secure home into life in a factory, and they diverge in predicting whether she will find happiness there, in spite of what they guess will be harsh conditions, or whether she will flee, returning to a simpler life on a farm.

 ## Responding to the Paterson Novels

With all of these concepts in mind, students set out to read Paterson's well-researched novel about a character whose grit and pride and strength make her a favorite of my students. While they read, they keep a journal in which they react to the book; when I've used other titles as the centerpiece for this unit, these reaction activities are the same:

- they respond to the plot and characters of the novel on a personal level;

- they pose questions to the author about anything that puzzles, delights, frustrates, or concerns them;

- they make connections of any sort—about plot, theme, characterization, characters and motivations, settings, narrative voice, tone—with their chosen title from the supplemental book list; and

- they highlight any passages that sound to them particularly American.

Note that I do not provide a definition of the term *American*. And I do not ask the students to do any research on how critics describe the characteristics of American literature. I do ask them to think about their high school reading experiences in their American literature survey course, or about any college reading experiences in American literature, and to compare *Lyddie* to other titles that are typically part of the high school curriculum. What connections do they see between *Lyddie* and any of those titles?

Different students have reflected on *Lyddie* by talking about titles as diverse as *The Autobiography of Benjamin Franklin* to *Of Mice and Men*, from *The Devil and Daniel Webster* to *Death of a Salesman*. Students have written about *The Scarlet Letter, The Awakening,* about James Fenimore Cooper and Sinclair Lewis. Poems have been referenced—by Sandburg, Thoreau, Stevens, Marianne Moore, and Whitman. In whatever comparisons they have made, students have brought their own experience of American literature to bear in ways that showed how, for them, *Lyddie* resonated in terms of theme, style, a sense of optimism or openness to the world and to change in ways that surprised me and pushed my own thinking about the defining characteristics of American literature. I ask them to list any facts or aspects of the novel reflective of the reality of the nineteenth-century Industrial Revolution that they might want to investigate or research.

When we come together to discuss *Lyddie*, the entire class participates in several activities. First, students generate categories of characters—and then argue about who goes into which category; for example, some of their category suggestions have included emotionally mature v. immature; gritty v. timid; agents of change v. reactors; malleable v. hardened; open v. stagnant; sympathetic v. not likeable. They create decision-making charts on which they list points at which Lyddie has to make critical decisions that affected the direction of the story line, brainstorm other options she had at those times, list the pros and cons of each choice, and decide, in the end, whether the choice Lyddie makes as described by Paterson makes sense given her character and the context of her life, especially as a woman. They regroup and skim essays by Paterson that I provide from *Gates of Excellence* ("Yes, But Is It True?") and *The Spying Heart* ("Hope and Happy Endings"), looking for information that added to their appreciation or understanding of this novel.

Over time students taking Children's and Young Adult Literature have identified traits that seemed to characterize American literature: the importance of individuality, the exploration of frontier, identity formation, forgiveness, the power of choice, a tone of optimism in the face of great hardship, and the use of an expansive canvas and setting. Each of these traits become headings placed on separate pieces of chart paper which are then taped on the walls around the room. In their groups, students next participate in a gallery walk, moving from chart to chart and making notes about two items: whether they agree with the heading as being a defining characteristic of American literature given their own reading histories and experiences, and ways in which *Lyddie* does or does not evidence that trait.

The Jigsaw Activity

Jigsaw Phase I
Then I introduce our jigsaw activity. When students enter class on the date when we are scheduled to begin our expert group activities, I give

them each a large index card. On the card, they write a very short, three-to five-sentence plot overview, a statement about the theme and thesis of the work, and notes about to which characters they most related, and a statement about what they liked or disliked most about the book. If any students have been unable to complete the card because they have not read as assigned, I direct them to the library for completion of the reading—after which they have an individualized activity to complete on their own time to earn the credit their peers received for participating in the expert groups. Fortunately, few students are ever unprepared; I sometimes use the discussion forum feature of BlackBoard, our electronic course management system, as the means to ensure, through reading student postings on their titles prior to the class, that everyone is ready to participate.

In class, I group students who have read the same title together in "expert groups." As a group, they review the plot and theme or thesis insights, and then they answer a series of questions, writing their responses on big sheets of chart paper that I provide along with markers of various colors. For some reason, chart paper and markers seem to be a motivator, and I find that having to *write* something, rather than just discussing a topic, helps the groups focus and come to consensus. They answer the following questions:

- Who are the major characters in the work? What are some adjectives you would use to describe them? What, if any, are the predicaments the characters bring upon themselves? (One interesting set of responses occurred in a group including a student taking a research methods class in the English Department in which they had been learning about Jungian criticism, and the student began to talk about archetypes, applying them to characters in *Lyddie*. In the future, I hope to introduce this concept and tell students a bit about the Jungian approach and then ask them to think about the characters in this way.)

- How do individual characters use their strengths to deal with these predicaments? What do they learn in the process of addressing them?

- What generalizations can you make about your author's style? What aspects of her or his use of language did you, as a reader, most enjoy? What kinds of literary devices did she or he often use? What was the effect on you, as a reader, of specific kinds of imagery or other literary devices? How would you say the author's style is or is not connected to the kind of themes he or she investigates, or the kind of mood created? How would you compare the way your author uses language to that of Paterson in *Lyddie* or to Cormier in *The Chocolate War*, which we read earlier in the term?

- To what age group, or to what kind of reader, do you think your book would most appeal and why? Are there readers who might not respond particularly positively to the work? Would you choose to use the book as an in-common reading for a whole class? Why or why not? If yes, in what grade, given local curricular content and goals, might you place it? How could you use your book in conjunction with a title typically taught in an American literature course? What questions would you ask your secondary students instead of these questions here? (Often I hear responses such as, "Should I use this book in the future with other eleventh-grade American literature students? Why or why not? If you were going to select one ten-page section of the novel to excerpt in the American literature anthology, which one would you choose and why? If you were going to recommend this novel to a younger sibling or students in a lower grade, perhaps eighth grade, what do you think would be the most challenging aspects of the novel for them to understand?")

- What is your personal response to the book? What is it about the author's style, craft, themes, settings, characters, that cause that response? (Stover 2006).

After the groups respond to these questions, I provide masking tape and they put their charts on the walls so that everyone in the class is able to access this information during phase two of the jigsaw activity.

The Jigsaw Activity Phase II

At this point, I mix students into new groups so that each group has representatives who have read at least five different titles from the original seven. As each expert shares a brief overview of his or her title, the other group members are charged with listening to find answers to the following questions. One group member records the collective responses to these queries on overhead acetates:

- What are the dominant themes of these works, given your admittedly limited knowledge base? Paterson says, in various essays in *Gates of Excellence* and in *A Sense of Wonder* that she writes about hope and love. Given your knowledge of her works, including *Lyddie, Jacob,* and *Bridge to Terabithia,* do you think she is telling the truth? Do you think these two themes are important attributes of American literature? Of young adult literature? Why or why not? Love of what sort? Hope in what sense?

- Paterson says she writes to comfort a childhood self who was always an outsider. In what sense were the main characters in all your books outsiders?

- Lyddie is clearly shaped by the environment—both the physical geography in which she comes of age and then the physical hardships of the mill, as well as by the psychological tenor of the times. How does the environment in which the characters from your books are living contribute to the creation of their personalities? Can we make any generalizations about the nature of the American landscape and the concept of pushing back frontiers of all sorts and the way characters develop in these titles?

- Do the writers share any stylistic commonalities? If so, is there any way these could be said to be American—or are they more likely to be shared characteristics of literature written specifically for and about young adults? Revisit your initial journal entries in which you compared Lyddie to other works of American literature with which you are familiar as you consider this question.

- And, in her essay, "Do I Dare Disturb the Universe?" Paterson has stated, "My primary task is to somehow find my way through the cacophony of reality to the harmony of truth" (1995, 246). What is the "cacophony of reality"? What is "the harmony of truth"? How, if at all, is this statement of purpose reflected in the books you have read by Paterson? By others authors you've read for this unit?

- Finally, many of these novels could be considered historical fiction. Given your readings and prior experience with this genre, what are the defining characteristics of it? What are the qualities of good historical fiction? What are the benefits of reading historical fiction?

 ## Individual Accountability

I ask reporters for each group to give that group's answers to a particular question or questions so that we are not overwhelmed by hearing from each group about the totality of their discussions. And then I introduce new questions drawn from Moore's overview of Bressler's 1994 set of queries designed to provide readers with a basis for a feminist inquiry: What is the gender of the author of your book? Can you tell anything about the author's attitude toward women and their place in society? What effect might the author's cultural experiences have on the way he or she depicts the lives of the characters in the novel? What roles, in general, do women play in the novel? What do the male characters think of the female characters? How do the women speak and use language, and is their use of language any different from that of the men? (Moore 1997, 119). We use *Lyddie* and *Jacob Have I Loved* as touchstones for thinking through these questions—and then also talk about the ways in which the students' personal experiences fill in any gaps left by the author, particularly in terms of how they respond to the ending of the novel. As Wolfgang Iser notes, "No author worth his salt will ever attempt to set the *whole* picture before his readers' 'eyes'" (1980, 57).

For homework, students write three paragraphs; in the first, they discuss which title described by someone in their group, other than *Lyddie* or the title they read individually, they would most want to include if given the chance to incorporate a young adult novel into an American literature course. In the second, they list the pros and cons of the jigsaw approach and how they could adapt it for use with students in the grade they hope to teach. The third paragraph includes their response to considering the novels from the standpoint of focusing on gender roles, and, again, must say how they, as teachers, could help students both recognize the differences in reading that may derive from the reader's gender and recognize the importance of considering an author's gender and the time frame in which a novel is written in reflecting on the portrayal of the characters.

Historical Fiction

The next day, we address the concept of *historical fiction*, comparing *Jacob Have I Loved* and *Lyddie* as exemplars of this genre. I tell the students something of Paterson's own research process in writing *Lyddie*. She relied heavily on the information found in a book about nineteenth-century mills by Hanna Josephson called *The Golden Threads: New England Mill Girls and Magnates* (1949), and took notes from Harriet H. Robinson's *Loom and Spindle: On Life Among the Early Mill Girls*, published in 1898. She read books on the underground railroad in Vermont, and one by Schlesigner, *The Age of Jackson* (1988). Paterson researched manners, politics, female labor reform advocates, and she also read a book on how to study women's lives and how to use primary source documents, which she then did in her writing. She used letters by mill girls now housed at the Museum of American Textiles in Lowell, MA— "These letters shaped the characters of the mill girls in Paterson's novel and gave a sense of reality to the drama of the girls' lives," reports Fisher (2001, 134). Paterson cites one letter by a girl to her father seeking permission to move from one job to another, where conditions seem better, where she says there is more "equality."

Paterson also watched a play about the mill girls, got materials for teachers about it, and walked the streets of Lowell, MA, to get a feel for the paths the girls would have taken. In short, she really did her homework to ensure *Lyddie* is faithful to the historical context Paterson is trying to evoke. As Fisher notes, "Printed non-fiction materials, like literature, are social in that they are written by others, some by living authors, some by authors long since past. They are evidence that social influences on an author's work occur not only in immediate interactions, but across distance and time through the medium of print" (2001, 135), and Paterson's use of these materials helps her novel resonate the lived experience of Lyddie in powerful ways.

As we talk about the concept of *historical fiction*, students ponder just what makes a text historical fiction. Is it the gap between when the author was writing and when the events of the book took place? Is it the gap between the date when the reader engages with the text and the date of the events in the book? Or, is it the gap between the date when a reader is reading and the date an author wrote about events that were, at that point, contemporary? I give them a section from Temple, Martinez, and Yokota's text (2006), which describes how historical fiction functions as a genre. We debate the question posed by these authors: "Should historical fiction serve as a springboard for learning about the past? Or should readers primarily be encouraged to read historical fiction for aesthetic purposes" (351). Tomlinson, Tunnell, and Richgels (1993) argue that reading historical fiction helps us develop historical empathy, helping us understand motivations and the lives of ordinary people so that historical events become grounded in daily activities we can comprehend.

When asked if any of her characters have ever surprised her, Paterson says Lyddie did (Schmidt 1997). "I was surprised that she became so grasping. . . . It dawned on me later that she became for a while a reflection of the greed of the mill owners. There is always a danger that one will become like one's enemy" (Paterson 2006b). Schmidt asked Paterson why she was so hard on Lyddie. Things crumble around her, but she still rejects the offer of Luke to marry. Paterson responded that she does not see it that way. "Oh, she comes back and marries him. I know it's not in the book, but that's what happens. She returns, marries Luke, and perhaps founds a library" (Schmidt 1997, 444).

Final Comments

At the end of our last class session on *Lyddie, Jacob Have I Loved*, and the American Novel unit I hand out index cards and ask participants to fill them out as exit slips. On the lined side, they write what they are taking away from our unit, and on the unlined side they list questions they still have, either about the books or about the pedagogy they have experienced. In terms of the pedagogy, they usually say they valued the experience of engaging in the jigsaw process and recognizing how both groups and individuals can be held accountable for the learning that happens in such a collaborative endeavor. In terms of the content with which they had been working, they often comment that they better understand the concept of *intertextuality* as a result of working in the jigsaw groups. They say their appreciation of Paterson's literary strengths has deepened, and several usually comment that they have gained insight on *Bridge to Terabithia* even though we have not dealt with that title explicitly in this discussion. They often note that they are walking away with a longer list of books to read during their next break, and many report that they feel they are beginning to understand what distinguishes American literature from that produced in other cultures and to appreciate how young adult titles can be used to help middle and high school students start to consider what makes literature American.

Choice and Invitation

Choice and invitation: These words summarize the lessons learned by all of us involved in this project on teaching selected works by Katherine Paterson. Students who are provided with rich, engaging, diversely appealing novels, who are given choices about how and what to read, who then have the time and space to read them can and do, sometimes against their will, find themselves grabbed by a character or a plot, pulled into another world, and forced by the individuals they meet in that world to think and feel and grow. Provided with opportunities to make sense of their reading in safe, inviting settings, collaborating with others who are also genuinely wrestling with the text, students can and do create meaningful relationships with texts in ways that help them learn about the art and craft of literature, the nature of different genres, the perspectives of others, and, of course, themselves. Asked to generate her own questions based on their reading of *The Preacher's Boy*, Ruth, from Mary's class, came up with a whole series of complexly interrelated queries about courage, including *How can showing courage change a person? How does age affect somebody's ability to be courageous? How are determination and courage related? Does it take skill to have courage? How do your friends affect courage? What really makes one courageous? What builds courage?* And Ruth and her peers had a discussion that ranged back and forth from the book to their own lives, as middle school students, that went far beyond the limits of what they would have answered had they been responding to questions—even good questions, such as these—generated by someone else, whether an anthology editor or a teacher.

When Paterson gave her acceptance speech for the Astrid Lindgrin Award, she quoted from her novel *The Same Stuff as Stars,* which tells the story of Angel, a young girl who has been discarded by society. Her dad's in jail; her mother has abandoned her and her little brother. But she finds herself looking up at the stars one night, hearing something that amazes her: She and the stars are made up of the same stuff. And knowing that, Angel's world is turned upside down. Paterson goes on to say,

> Jim Wallis, one of America's prophetic voices, tells a story of a young African American woman from Washington, DC named Lisa Sullivan who earned a Ph.D. at Yale, and then felt called to work in the city with forgotten children of color. She died at a tragically young age, though her legacy lives on in the young people she inspired and counseled. But, Wallis, said, "There is one thing [Lisa] often said to them and to all of us that has stayed with me. . . . When people would complain, as they often do, that we don't have any leaders today—or ask 'where are the Martin Luther Kings now?'—Lisa would get angry. And she would declare: 'We are the ones we have been waiting for.'"
>
> So maybe that's the answer to my question, Why me? Why us? Because we are the ones we've been waiting for. What I want to say to isolated, angry, fearful youth—to all the children society has regarded as disposable, children who cannot love others because they have not yet learned to love themselves, all the sad, the lonely, the frightened who might read my books is this: you are seen, you are not alone, you are not despised, you are unique and of infinite value in the human family. As a writer I can try to say this through the words of a story, but it is up to each of us who come into contact with these children every day in our homes, our schools, our communities and as citizens of this broken world—it is up to us to embody those words—to become their Maime Trotters, their star men—we, each of us, are the word of hope become flesh. (2006a)

Choice and invitation, too, can be used to describe the qualities of Paterson's works that engage students so eagerly in reading. Her characters, all outsiders in the worlds in which they find themselves, make choices that, in the end, bring them to a place of satisfaction. They and their readers know that they will be OK. And because, like Paterson herself, her characters understand the importance of reaching out to help others, they then invite those about whom they care—as well as their readers—to come with them into their newfound sense of grace. It is our job, as teachers, to help Paterson's characters perform this most important task for their readers, our students.

BIBLIOGRAPHY

Katherine Paterson's Works

Titles preceded by an asterisk indicate novels referenced in this book.

Chapter Books and Novels for Children and Young Adults

Bread and Roses, Too. 2006. New York: Clarion.

* *Bridge to Terabithia.* 1987. New York: HarperTrophy.

*Come Sing, Jimmy Jo. 1995. New York: Puffin.

Flip-Flop Girl. 1994. New York: Dutton.

*The Great Gilly Hopkins. 2004. New York: HarperTrophy.

*Jacob Have I Loved. 1980. New York: HarperTrophy.

Jip, His Story. 1990. New York: Lodestar.

*Lyddie. 1992. New York: Puffin.

The Master Puppeteer. 1975. Illustrations by Haru Wells. New York: Crowell.

Of Nightingales That Weep. 1974. Illustrations by Haru Wells. New York: Crowell.

*Park's Quest. 1989. New York: Puffin.

*Preacher's Boy. 2001. New York: HarperTrophy.

Rebels of the Heavenly Kingdom. 1983. New York: Dutton.

*The Sign of the Chrysanthemum. 1988. New York: HarperTrophy.

Children's Chapter and Picture Books

The Angel and the Donkey. (Retelling). 1996. Illustrations by Alexander Koshkin. New York: Clarion.

Blueberries for the Queen. 2004. With John Paterson. Illustrations by Susan Jeffers. New York: HarperCollins.

Celia, and Sweet, Sweet Water. 1998. Illustrations by Vladimir Vagin. New York: Clarion.

*The Field of the Dogs. 2002. New York: HarperTrophy.

The King's Equal. 1999. Illustrations by Curtis Woodbridge. New York: HarperTrophy.

Marvin One Too Many. 2001. Images by Jane Clark Brown. New York: HarperCollins.

Marvin's Best Christmas Present Ever. 1997. Illustrations by Jane Clark Brown. New York: HarperCollins.

Parzival: The Quest of the Grail Knight. (Retelling). 1998. New York: Lodestar.

*The Same Stuff as Stars. 2002. New York: Clarion.

The Smallest Cow in the World. 1991. Illustrations by Jane Clark Brown. New York: HarperCollins.

The Wide-Awake Princess. 2000. Illustrations by Vladimir Vagin. New York: Clarion.

Christmas Stories

Angels and Other Strangers: Family Christmas Stories. 1979. New York: Crowell.

A Midnight Clear: Stories for the Christmas Season. 1995. New York: Lodestar.

Nonfiction and Essays

Consider the Lilies: Plants of the Bible. With John Paterson. 1986. Paintings by Anne Ophelia Dowden. New York: Crowell.

Gates of Excellence: On Reading and Writing Books for Children. 1981. New York: Elsevier/Nelson Books.

Images of God. 1998. With John Paterson. Illustrations by Alexander Koshkin. New York: Clarion.

The Invisible Child: On Reading and Writing Books for Children. 2001. New York: Dutton.

A Sense of Wonder: On Reading and Writing Books for Children. 1995. New York: Plume.

The Spying Heart: More Thoughts on Reading and Writing Books for Children. 1989. New York: Lodestar.

Who Am I? 1992. Grand Rapids, MI: Eerdman.

WORKS CITED

Entries preceded by an asterisk are particularly useful in the Katherine Paterson Literature Circles Project.

Beech, Linda Ward. 1996. *Scholastic Literature Guide Grades 4–8:* Bridge to Terabithia *by Katherine Paterson.* New York: Scholastic.

Beers, Kylene. 2006. "Closing the Reading Achievement Gap: Strategies That Accelerate Reading and Writing Abilities in Underachieving Middle and High School Students." Presentation at the National Council of Teachers of English Conference, 19 November, Nashville, TN.

Burnett, Francis. 1910. *The Secret Garden.* Philadelphia: Lippincott.

The Class of the 20th Century: 1940–1952. Vols. 3 and 4. 1998. A&E Home Video. Videocassette.

Colorado, Desirae, and Kendra Perkins. 2006. "Interview with Katherine Paterson." http://content.scholastic.com/browse/article.jsp?id=8083&FullBreadCrumb=%3Ca+href%3D%22%2Fbrowse%2Fsearch.jsp%3Fquery%3DKatherine+Paterson%26c1%3DCONTENT30%26c2%3Dfalse%22%3EAll+Results+%3C%2Fa%3E. Accessed April 23, 2007.

"Contributor Biography of Katherine Paterson." n.d. http://content.scholastic.com/browse/contributor.jsp?id=3555&FullBreadCrumb=%3Ca+href%3D%22%2Fbrowse%2Fsearch.jsp%3Fquery%3DKatherine+Paterson%26c1%3DCONTENT30%26c2%3Dfalse%22%3EAll+Results+%3C%2Fa%3E. Accessed April 23, 2007.

Conversations with Betsy Gardiner, Kathy Slingland, Mary Christensen by
        Lois Stover. Various dates, September 2004–October, 2006.
Cormier, Robert. 1986. *The Chocolate War*. New York: Laurel Leaf.
———. 2000. *Heroes*. New York: Laurel Leaf.
Crutcher, Chris. 2003. *Staying Fat for Sarah Byrnes*. New York: HarperTempest.
Daniels, Harvey. 2002. *Literature Circles: Voice and Choice in Book Clubs and
        Reading Groups*. Portland, ME: Stenhouse.
Dewey, John. 1897. *My Pedagogic Creed*. In *John Dewey: The Early Works,
        1882–1898*. Vol. 5. Ed. Jo Ann Boydston. Carbondale: Southern Illinois
        University Press, 1972.
———. 1916. *Democracy and Education*. In *John Dewey: The Middle Works,
        1899–1924*. Vol. 9. Ed. Jo Ann Boydston. Carbondale: Southern Illinois
        University Press, 1985.
———. 1938. *Experience and Education*. In *John Dewey: The Later Works,
        1925–1953*. Vol. 13. Ed. Jo Ann Boydston. Carbondale: Southern Illinois
        University Press, 1991.
Fireside, Byrna J. 1978. "Two Orphans Without Mothers." *New York Times*,
        April 3.
Fisher, Bonnie. 2001. *Social Influences on the Writing of Marion Dane Bauer and
        Katherine Paterson: Writing as a Social Act*. Lewiston, NY: Edwin Mellon
        Press.
Flower, Linda. 1994. *The Construction of Negotiated Meaning: A Social Cognitive
        Theory of Writing*. Carbondale: Southern Illinois University Press.
Hesse, Karen. 1997. *Out of the Dust*. New York: Scholastic/Apple Signature
        Edition.
Iser, Wolfgang. 1980. "The Reading Process: A Phenomenological Approach."
        In *Reader-Response Criticism: From Formalism to Post-Structuralism*. Ed.
        Jane Tompkins, 50–69. Baltimore: Johns Hopkins University Press.
Johnson, Virginia. 2004. "Katherine Paterson's Healing Words." www
        .kidspoint.org/columns2.asp?column_id=10828&column_type=
        author. Accessed February 2, 2006.
Jones, Linda T. 1981. "Profile: Katherine Paterson." *Language Arts* 58 (2): 195.
Josephson, Hanna. 1949. *The Golden Threads: New England Mill Girls and
        Magnates*. New York: Duell, Slona, and Pearce.
Joyce, Bruce, Marsha Weil, and Emily Calhoun. 2003. *Models of Teaching*. 7th
        ed. Boston: Allyn & Bacon.

Kjelle, Marylou Morano. 2005. *Classic Storytellers: Katherine Paterson.* Hickessin, DE: Michael Lane Publishers.

Knoblauch, C. H., and Lil Brannon. 1993. *Critical Teaching and the Idea of Literacy.* Portsmouth, NH: Boynton/Cook.

Landes, Sonia. 1989. "The Poetry of Chapter Titles." *The New Advocate* 2 (3): 159–68.

Lee, Harper. 1960. *To Kill a Mockingbird.* Philadelphia: Lippincott.

Lockhart, Robert. 1998. "Validating the Personal in Katherine Paterson." *The ALAN Review* 25 (2): 8–15.

McGinty, Alice B. 2005. *Katherine Paterson.* New York: Rosen.

*Moore, John Noell. 1997. *Interpreting Young Adult Literature: Literary Theory in the Secondary Classroom.* Portsmouth, NH: Boynton/Cook.

*Morris, Catherine, and Inez Ramsey. n.d. "Katherine Paterson Teacher Resource File." *The Internet School Library Media Center Katherine Paterson Page.* http://falcon.jmu.edu/~ramseyil/paterson.htm. Accessed April 23, 2007.

Namovicz, Gene I. 1981. "Katherine Paterson." *Horn Book* 57 (4): 394–99.

Naylor, Phyllis Reynolds. 1993. *The Year of the Gopher.* New York: Laurel Leaf.

Nystrand, Martin. 1989. "A Social-Interactive Model of Writing." *Written Communication* 6 (1): 66–85.

Park, Barbara. 2006. *Skinny Bones.* New York: Yearling.

Paterson, Katherine. n.d. *The Author's Eye.* Random House. Videocassette.

———. 1981. *Gates of Excellence: On Reading and Writing Books for Children.* New York: E. P. Dutton (Lodestar).

———. 1982. "The Aim of the Writer Who Writes for Children." *Theory into Practice* 21 (4): 325–31.

———. 1987. *Bridge to Terabithia.* New York: HarperTrophy.

———. 1989. *The Spying Heart.* New York: Crowell.

———. 1990. *Stick to Reality and a Dream.* Washington, DC: Children's Literature Center, Library of Congress.

———. 1995a. "Do I Dare Disturb the Universe?" In *A Sense of Wonder: On Reading and Writing Books for Children.* New York: Plume.

*———. 1995b. *A Sense of Wonder: On Reading and Writing Books for Children.* New York: Plume.

———. 2001a. *The Invisible Child: On Reading and Writing Books for Children.* New York: Dutton.

———. 2001b. *The Preacher's Boy*. New York: HarperTrophy.

———. 2006a. "Astrid Lindgren Lecture." June, 2006. www.alma.se/page.php ?realm=625. Accessed April 23, 2007.

———. 2006b. "The Official Website of Katherine Paterson." www .terabithia.com/about.html. Accessed April 23, 2007.

———. 2006c. "Swedish Parliament Speech." June 1, 2006. www.alma.se/page.php?realm=629. Accessed April 23, 2007.

Paton, Alan. 1951. *Cry, the Beloved Country*. New York: Scribner's.

Peterson, Eric. "Katherine Paterson: A Biography." www.ulster.net /~petersne/bio.htm. Accessed February 2, 2006.

Rawlings, Marjorie Kinnan. 1938. *The Yearling*. New York: Scribner's.

Robinson, Harriet H. 1898. *Loom and Spindle: On Life Among the Early Mill Girls*. New York: Thomas J. Crowell.

Rochman, Hazel. 1996. "Review of *Jip*." *Booklist* 93 (1): 1.

Rosenblatt, Louise M. 1994. *The Reader, the Text, the Poem: The Transactional Theory of the Literary Work*. Carbondale: Southern Illinois University Press.

———. 1995. *Literature as Exploration*. 5th ed. New York: Modern Language Association of America.

Sanderson, Jeannette. 2004. *Scholastic BookFiles: A Reading Guide to* Bridge to Terabithia *by Katherine Paterson*. New York: Scholastic.

Schlesigner, Arthur M. 1988. *The Age of Jackson*. Boston: Back Bay Books.

Schlick Noe, Katherine L., and Nancy J. Johnson. 1999. *Getting Started with Literature Circles*. Norwood, MA: Christopher-Gordon Publishers.

*Schmidt, Gary D. 1994. *Presenting Katherine Paterson*. New York: Twayne.

———. 1997. "Katherine Paterson." In *Writers for Young Adults*. Ed. Ted Hipple, 444–54. New York: Charles Scribner's Sons.

Sendak, Maurice. 1981. *Outside Over There*. New York: Harper.

Settle, Mary Lee. 1977. *Bloodtie*. Boston: Houghton Mifflin.

Slavin, Robert E. 1995. *Cooperative Learning*. 2d ed. Boston: Allyn & Bacon.

Stowe, Harriet Beecher. 1996. *Uncle Tom's Cabin*. New York: Modern Library Editions.

Stover, Lois T. 1996. *Young Adult Literature: The Heart of the Middle School Curriculum*. Portsmouth, NH: Boynton/Cook.

———. 2006. "Teaching *Out of the Dust* as an American Novel." *Notes on American Literature* 16 (2): 4–6.

*Sutton, Roger. 2001. "An Interview with Katherine Paterson." *Horn Book* 77 (6): 689–99.

Taylor, Mildred. 2003. *The Land*. New York: Puffin.

Temple, Charles, Mariam Martinez, and Junko Yokota. 2006. *Children's Books in Children's Hands: An Introduction to Their Literature*. 3d ed. Boston: Pearson/Allyn & Bacon.

Thralls, C., and N. R. Blyler. 1993. "The Social Perspective and Pedagogy in Technical Communication." *Technical Communication Quarterly* 2: 249–70.

Tomlinson, Carl M., Michael O. Tunnell, and Donald J. Richgels. 1993. "The Content and Writing of History in Textbooks and Trade Books." In *The Story of Ourselves: Teaching History Through Children's Literature*. Ed. Michael O. Tunnell and Richard Ammon, 51–62. Portsmouth, NH: Heinemann.

Voigt, Cynthia. 2003. *A Solitary Blue*. New York: Aladdin.

Wilde, Susan. 1993. "Katherine Paterson: On Writing a Different Kind of Happily-Ever-After Story." *Bookpage* (March): 8.

Woodson, Jacqueline. 2002. *Hush*. New York: Putnam.

Woolfolk, Anita. 2004. *Educational Psychology*. 9th ed. Boston: Pearson.

Yagawa, Sumiko. 1981. *The Crane Wife*. Trans. Katherine Paterson. New York: Morrow.